MEDIA, FEMINISM, CULTURAL STUDIES

Stepping Forward: Essays, Lectures and Interviews
by Wolfgang Iser

Wild Zones: Pornography, Art and Feminism
by Kelly Ives

The Sacred Cinema of Andrei Tarkovsky
by Jeremy Mark Robinson

Liv Tyler
by Thomas A. Christie

Women In the Fine Arts
By Clara Erskine Clement

The Madonna In Art
By Estelle Hurll

The Cinema of Richard Linklater
by Thomas A. Christie

The Cinema of Hayao Miyazaki
Jeremy Mark Robinson

'Cosmo Woman': The World of Women's Magazines
by Oliver Whitehorne

The Art of Katsuhiro Otomo
By Jeremy Mark Robinson

Walerian Borowczyk
by Jeremy Mark Robinson

Andrea Dworkin
by Jeremy Mark Robinson

Cixous, Irigaray, Kristeva: The Jouissance of French Feminism
by Kelly Ives

Erotic Art In the 19th Century
By Cassidy Hughes

Erotic Art In the Renaissance
By Cassidy Hughes

Erotic Art
By Cassidy Hughes

Detonation Britain: Nuclear War in the UK
by Jeremy Mark Robinson

The Erotic Object: Sexuality in Sculpture From Prehistory to the Present Day
by Susan Quinnell

Women in Pop Music
by Helen Challis

Julia Kristeva: Art, Love, Melancholy, Philosophy, Semiotics
by Kelly Ives

Luce Irigaray: Lips, Kissing, and the Politics of Sexual Difference
by Kelly Ives

Helene Cixous I Love You: The Jouissance *of Writing*
by Kelly Ives

ARTHUR SCHOPENHAUER

ESSAYS

THE ART OF LITERATURE

ARTHUR SCHOPENHAUER

ESSAYS

THE ART OF LITERATURE

TRANSLATED BY
T. BAILEY SAUNDERS, M.A.

EDITED BY JEREMY MARK ROBINSON

CRESCENT MOON

First published 1893. This edition © 2021. Reprint 2024.

Set in Book Antiqua 10 on 14pt.
Designed by Radiance Graphics.

Thanks to the authors and publishers quoted.

British Library Cataloguing in Publication data

ISBN-13 9781861718181
ISBN-13 9781861719003

CRESCENT MOON PUBLISHING
P.O. Box 1312, Maidstone, Kent, ME14 5XU
Great Britain, www.crmoon.com

CONTENTS

NOTE ON THE TEXT

The text is from *The Essays of Arthur Schopenhauer* by Arthur Schopenhauer, translated by T. Bailey Saunders, published by A.L. Burt, New York, 1893. The *Biographical Note* is from *Essays of Schopenhauer*, translated by Mrs Rudolf Dircks, Scott Library, 1920.

Footnotes are in square brackets [1]

Arthur Schopenhauer by Ludwig Sigismund Ruhl, 1815

Arthur Schopenhauer

TRANSLATOR'S PREFACE

The contents of this, as of the other volumes in the series, have been drawn from Schopenhauer's *Parerga,* and amongst the various subjects dealt with in that famous collection of essays, Literature holds an important place. Nor can Schopenhauer's opinions fail to be of special value when he treats of literary form and method. For, quite apart from his philosophical pretensions, he claims recognition as a great writer; he is, indeed, one of the best of the few really excellent prose-writers of whom Germany can boast. While he is thus particularly qualified to speak of Literature as an Art, he has also something to say upon those influences which, outside of his own merits, contribute so much to an author's success, and are so often undervalued when he obtains immediate popularity. Schopenhauer's own sore experiences in the matter of reputation lend an interest to his remarks upon that subject, although it is too much to ask of human nature that he should approach it in any dispassionate spirit.

In the following pages we have observations upon style by one who was a stylist in the best sense of the word, not affected, nor yet a phrasemonger; on thinking for oneself by a philosopher who never did anything else; on criticism by a writer who suffered much from the inability of others to understand him; on reputation by a candidate who, during the greater part of his life, deserved without obtaining it; and on genius by one who was incontestably of the privileged order himself. And whatever may be thought of some of his opinions on matters of detail - on anonymity, for instance, or on the question whether good work is never done for money - there can be no doubt that his general view of literature, and the conditions under which it flourishes, is perfectly sound.

It might be thought, perhaps, that remarks which were meant to apply to the German language would have but little bearing upon one so different from it as English. This would be a just objection if Schopenhauer treated literature in a petty spirit, and confined himself to pedantic inquiries into matters of grammar and etymology, or mere niceties of phrase. But this is not so. He deals with his subject broadly, and takes large and general views; nor can anyone who knows anything of the philosopher suppose this to mean that he is vague and feeble. It is true that now and again in the course of these essays he makes remarks which are obviously meant to apply to the failings of certain writers of his own age and country; but in such a case I have generally given his sentences a turn, which, while keeping them faithful to the spirit of the original, secures for them a less restricted range, and makes Schopenhauer a critic of similar faults in whatever age or country they may appear. This has been done in spite of a sharp word on page seventeen of this volume, addressed to translators who dare to revise their author; but the change is one with which not even Schopenhauer could quarrel.

It is thus a significant fact - a testimony to the depth of his insight and, in the main, the justice of his opinions - that views of literature which appealed to his own immediate contemporaries, should be found to hold good elsewhere and at a distance of fifty years. It means that what he had to say was worth saying; and since it is adapted thus equally to diverse times and audiences, it is probably of permanent interest.

The intelligent reader will observe that much of the charm of

Schopenhauer's writing comes from its strongly personal character, and that here he has to do, not with a mere maker of books, but with a man who thinks for himself and has no false scruples in putting his meaning plainly upon the page, or in unmasking sham wherever he finds it. This is nowhere so true as when he deals with literature; and just as in his treatment of life, he is no flatterer to men in general, so here he is free and outspoken on the peculiar failings of authors. At the same time he gives them good advice. He is particularly happy in recommending restraint in regard to reading the works of others, and the cultivation of independent thought; and herein he recalls a saying attributed to Hobbes, who was not less distinguished as a writer than as a philosopher, to the effect that *"if he had read as much as other men, he should have been as ignorant as they."*

Schopenhauer also utters a warning, which we shall do well to take to heart in these days, against mingling the pursuit of literature with vulgar aims. If we follow him here, we shall carefully distinguish between literature as an object of life and literature as a means of living, between the real love of truth and beauty, and that detestable false love which looks to the price it will fetch in the market. I am not referring to those who, while they follow a useful and honorable calling in bringing literature before the public, are content to be known as men of business. If, by the help of some second witch of Endor, we could raise the ghost of Schopenhauer, it would be interesting to hear his opinion of a certain kind of literary enterprise which has come into vogue since his day, and now receives an amount of attention very much beyond its due. We may hazard a guess at the direction his opinion would take. He would doubtless show us how this enterprise, which is carried on by self-styled *literary men,* ends by making literature into a form of merchandise, and treating it as though it were so much goods to be bought and sold at a profit, and most likely to produce quick returns if the maker's name is well known. Nor would it be the ghost of the real Schopenhauer unless we heard a vigorous denunciation of men who claim a connection with literature by a servile flattery of successful living authors – the dead cannot be made to pay – in the hope of appearing to advantage in their reflected light and turning that advantage into money.

In order to present the contents of this book in a convenient form, I have not scrupled to make an arrangement with the chapters somewhat different from that which exists in the original; so that two or more subjects which are there dealt with successively in one and the same chapter, here stand by themselves. In consequence of this, some of the titles of the sections are not to be found in the original. I may state, however, that the essays on *Authorship* and *Style* and the latter part of that on *Criticism* are taken direct from the chapter headed *Ueber Schriftstellerei und Stil*; and that the remainder of the essay on *Criticism*, with that of *Reputation*, is supplied by the remarks *Ueber Urtheil, Kritik, Beifall und Ruhm*. The essays on *The Study of Latin*, on *Men of Learning*, and on *Some Forms of Literature*, are taken chiefly from the four sections *Ueber Gelehrsamkeit und Gelehrte, Ueber Sprache und Worte, Ueber Lesen und Bücher: Anhang*, and *Zur Metaphysik des Schönen*. The essay on *Thinking for Oneself* is a rendering of certain remarks under the heading *Selbstdenken*. *Genius* was a favorite subject of speculation with Schopenhauer, and he often touches upon it in the course of his works; always, however, to put forth the same theory in regard to it as may be found in the concluding section of this volume. Though the essay has little or nothing to do with literary method, the subject of which it treats is the most needful element of success in literature; and I have introduced it on that ground. It forms part of a chapter in the *Parerga* entitled *Den Intellekt überhaupt und in jeder Beziehung betreffende Gedanken: Anhang verwandter Stellen*.

It has also been part of my duty to invent a title for this volume; and I am well aware that objection may be made to the one I have chosen, on the ground that in common language it is unusual to speak of literature as an art, and that to do so is unduly to narrow its meaning and to leave out of sight its main function as the record of thought. But there is no reason why the word *Literature* should not be employed in that double sense which is allowed to attach to *Painting, Music, Sculpture,* as signifying either the objective outcome of a certain mental activity, seeking to express itself in outward form; or else the particular kind of mental activity in question, and the methods it follows. And we do, in fact, use it in this latter sense, when we say of a writer that he pursues literature as a calling. If, then, literature can be taken to mean a process as well as a result of mental activity, there can be no error in speaking of it as Art. I use that term in its broad sense, as meaning skill in the display of thought; or, more fully, a right use of the rules of applying to the practical exhibition of thought, with whatever material it may deal. In connection with literature, this is a sense and an application of the term which have been sufficiently established by the example of the great writers of antiquity.

It may be asked, of course, whether the true thinker, who will always form the soul of the true author, will not be so much occupied with what he has to say, that it will appear to him a trivial thing to spend great effort on embellishing the form in which he delivers it. Literature, to be worthy of the name, must, it is true, deal with noble matter - the riddle of our existence, the great facts of life, the changing passions of the human heart, the discernment of some deep moral truth. It is easy to lay too much stress upon the mere garment of thought; to be too precise; to give to the arrangement of words an attention that should rather be paid to the promotion of fresh ideas. A writer who makes this mistake is like a fop who spends his little mind in adorning his person. In short, it may be charged against the view of literature which is taken in calling it an Art, that, instead of making truth and insight the author's aim, it favors sciolism and a fantastic and affected style. There is, no doubt, some justice in the objection; nor have we in our own day, and especially amongst younger men, any lack of writers who endeavor to win confidence, not by adding to the stock of ideas in the world, but by despising the use of plain language. Their faults are not new in the history of literature; and it is a pleasing sign of Schopenhauer's insight that a merciless exposure of them, as they existed half a century ago, is still quite applicable to their modern form.

And since these writers, who may, in the slang of the hour, be called "impressionists" in literature, follow their own bad taste in the manufacture of dainty phrases, devoid of all nerve, and generally with some quite commonplace meaning, it is all the more necessary to discriminate carefully between artifice and art.

But although they may learn something from Schopenhauer's advice, it is not chiefly to them that it is offered. It is to that great mass of writers, whose business is to fill the columns of the newspapers and the pages of the review, and to produce the ton of novels that appear every year. Now that almost everyone who can hold a pen aspires to be called an author, it is well to emphasize the fact that literature is an art in some respects more important than any other. The problem of this art is the discovery of those qualities of style and treatment which entitled any work to be called good literature.

It will be safe to warn the reader at the very outset that, if he wishes to avoid being led astray, he should in his search for these qualities turn to books that have stood the test of time.

For such an amount of hasty writing is done in these days that it is really difficult for anyone who reads much of it to avoid contracting its faults, and thus gradually coming to terms of dangerous familiarity with bad methods. This advice will be especially needful if things that have little or no claim to be called literature at all - the newspapers, the monthly magazine, and the last new tale of intrigue or adventure - fill a large measure, if not the whole, of the time given to reading. Nor are those who are sincerely anxious to have the best thought in the best language quite free from danger if they give too much attention to the contemporary authors, even though these seem to think and write excellently. For one generation alone is incompetent to decide upon the merits of any author whatever; and as literature, like all art, is a thing of human invention, so it can be pronounced good only if it obtains lasting admiration, by establishing a permanent appeal to mankind's deepest feeling for truth and beauty.

It is in this sense that Schopenhauer is perfectly right in holding that neglect of the ancient classics, which are the best of all models in the art of writing, will infallibly lead to a degeneration of literature.

And the method of discovering the best qualities of style, and of forming a theory of writing, is not to follow some trick or mannerism that happens to please for the moment, but to study the way in which great authors have done their best work.

It will be said that Schopenhauer tells us nothing we did not know before. Perhaps so; as he himself says, the best things are seldom new. But he puts the old truths in a fresh and forcible way; and no one who knows anything of good literature will deny that these truths are just now of very fit application.

It was probably to meet a real want that, a year or two ago, an ingenious person succeeded in drawing a great number of English and American writers into a confession of their literary creed and the art they adopted in authorship; and the interesting volume in which he gave these confessions to the world contained some very good advice, although most of it had been said before in different forms. More recently a new departure, of very doubtful use, has taken place; and two books have been issued, which aim, the one at being an author's manual, the other at giving hints on essays and how to write them.

A glance at these books will probably show that their authors have still something to learn.

Both of these ventures seem, unhappily, to be popular; and, although they may claim a position next-door to that of the present volume I beg to say that it has no connection with them whatever. Schopenhauer does not attempt to teach the art of making bricks without straw.

I wish to take this opportunity of tendering my thanks to a large number of reviewers for the very gratifying reception given to the earlier volumes of this series. And I have great pleasure in expressing my obligations to my friend Mr. W.G. Collingwood, who has looked over most of my proofs and often given me excellent advice in my effort to turn Schopenhauer into readable English.

T.B.S.

BIOGRAPHICAL NOTE

By Mrs Rudolf Dircks[1]

Arthur Schopenhauer was born at No. 117 of the Heiligengeist Strasse, at Dantzic, on February 22, 1788. His parents on both sides traced their descent from Dutch ancestry, the great-grandfather of his mother having occupied some ecclesiastical position at Gorcum. Dr. Gwinner in his *Life* does not follow the Dutch ancestry on the father's side, but merely states that the great-grandfather of Schopenhauer at the beginning of the eighteenth century rented a farm, the Stuthof, in the neighbourhood of Dantzic. This ancestor, Andreas Schopenhauer, received here on one occasion an unexpected visit from Peter the Great and Catherine, and it is related that there being no stove in the chamber which the royal pair selected for the night, their host, for the purpose of heating it, set fire to several small bottles of brandy which had been emptied on the stone floor. His son Andreas followed in the footsteps of his father, combining a commercial career with country pursuits. He died in 1794 at Ohra, where he had purchased an estate, and to which he had retired to spend his closing years. His wife (the grandmother of Arthur) survived him for some years, although shortly after his death she was declared insane and incapable of managing her affairs. This couple had

1 From *Essays of Schopenhauer*, translated by Mrs Rudolf Dircks, Scott Library, 1920.

four sons: the eldest, Michael Andreas, was weak-minded; the second, Karl Gottfried, was also mentally weak and had deserted his people for evil companions; the youngest son, Heinrich Floris, possessed, however, in a considerable degree the qualities which his brothers lacked. He possessed intelligence, a strong character, and had great commercial sagacity; at the same time, he took a definite interest in intellectual pursuits, reading Voltaire, of whom he was more or less a disciple, and other French authors, possessing a keen admiration for English political and family life, and furnishing his house after an English fashion. He was a man of fiery temperament and his appearance was scarcely prepossessing; he was short and stout; he had a broad face and turned-up nose, and a large mouth. This was the father of our philosopher.

When he was thirty-eight, Heinrich Schopenhauer married, on May 16, 1785, Johanna Henriette Trosiener, a young lady of eighteen, and daughter of a member of the City Council of Dantzic. She was at this time an attractive, cultivated young person, of a placid disposition, who seems to have married more because marriage offered her a comfortable settlement and assured position in life, than from any passionate affection for her wooer, which, it is just to her to say, she did not profess. Heinrich Schopenhauer was so much influenced by English ideas that he desired that his first child should be born in England; and thither, some two years after their marriage, the pair, after making a *détour* on the Continent, arrived. But after spending some weeks in London Mrs. Schopenhauer was seized with home-sickness, and her husband acceded to her entreaties to return to Dantzic, where a child, the future philosopher, was shortly afterwards born. The first five years of the child's life were spent in the country, partly at the Stuthof which had formerly belonged to Andreas Schopenhauer, but had recently come into the possession of his maternal grandfather.

Five years after the birth of his son, Heinrich Schopenhauer, in consequence of the political crisis, which he seems to have taken keenly to heart, in the affairs of the Hanseatic town of Dantzic, transferred his business and his home to Hamburg, where in 1795 a second child, Adele, was born. Two years later, Heinrich, who intended to train his son for a business life, took him, with this idea, to Havre, by way of Paris, where they spent a little time, and left him there with M. Grégoire, a commercial connection. Arthur remained at Havre for two years, receiving private instruction with this man's son Anthime, with whom he struck up a strong friendship, and when he returned to Hamburg it was found that he remembered but few words of his mother-tongue. Here he was placed in one of the principal private schools, where he remained for three years. Both his parents, but especially his mother, cultivated at this time the society of literary people, and entertained at their house Klopstock and other notable persons. In the summer following his return home from Havre he accompanied his parents on a continental tour, stopping amongst other places at Weimar, where he saw Schiller. His mother, too, had considerable literary tastes, and a distinct literary gift which, later, she cultivated to some advantage, and which brought her in the production of accounts of travel and fiction a not inconsiderable reputation. It is, therefore, not surprising that literary tendencies began to show themselves in her son, accompanied by a growing distaste for the career of commerce which his father wished him to follow. Heinrich Schopenhauer, although deprecating these tendencies, considered the question of purchasing a canonry for his son, but ultimately gave up the idea on the score of expense. He then proposed to take him on an extended trip to France, where he might meet his young friend Anthime, and then to England, if he would give up the idea of a literary calling, and the proposal was accepted.

In the spring of 1803, then, he accompanied his parents to London, where, after spending some time in sight-seeing, he was placed in the school of Mr. Lancaster at Wimbledon. Here he remained for three months, from July to September, laying the foundation of his knowledge of the English language, while his parents proceeded to Scotland. English formality, and what he conceived to be English hypocrisy, did not contrast favourably with his earlier and gayer experiences in France, and made an extremely unfavourable impression upon his mind; which found expression in letters to his friends and to his mother.

On returning to Hamburg after this extended excursion abroad, Schopenhauer was placed in the office of a Hamburg senator called Jenisch, but he was as little inclined as ever to follow a commercial career, and secretly shirked his work so that he might pursue his studies. A little later a somewhat unexplainable calamity occurred. When Dantzic ceased to be a free city, and Heinrich Schopenhauer at a considerable cost and monetary sacrifice transferred his business to Hamburg, the event caused him much bitterness of spirit. At Hamburg his business seems to have undergone fluctuations. Whether these further affected his spirit is not sufficiently established, but it is certain, however, that he developed peculiarities of manner, and that his temper became more violent. At any rate, one day in April 1805 it was found that he had either fallen or thrown himself into the canal from an upper storey of a granary; it was generally concluded that it was a case of suicide.

Schopenhauer was seventeen at the time of this catastrophe, by which he was naturally greatly affected. Although by the death of his father the influence which impelled him to a commercial career was removed, his veneration for the dead man remained with him through life, and on one occasion found expression in a curious tribute to his memory in a dedication (which was not, however, printed) to the second edition of *Die Welt als Wille und Vorstellung.* "That I could make use of and cultivate in a right direction the powers which nature gave me," he concludes, "that I could follow my natural impulse and think and work for countless others without the help of any one; for that I thank thee, my father, thank thy activity, thy cleverness, thy thrift and care for the future. Therefore I praise thee, my noble father. And every one who from my work derives any pleasure, consolation, or instruction shall hear thy name and know that if Heinrich Floris Schopenhauer had not been the man he was, Arthur Schopenhauer would have been a hundred times ruined."

The year succeeding her husband's death, Johanna Schopenhauer removed with her daughter to Weimar, after having attended to the settlement of her husband's affairs, which left her in possession of a considerable income. At Weimar she devoted herself to the pursuit of literature, and held twice a week a sort of salon, which was attended by Goethe, the two Schlegels, Wieland, Heinrich Meyer, Grimm, and other literary persons of note. Her son meanwhile continued for another year at the "dead timber of the desk," when his mother, acting under the advice of her friend Fernow, consented, to his great joy, to his following his literary bent.

During the next few years we find Schopenhauer devoting himself assiduously to acquiring the equipment for a learned career; at first at the Gymnasium at Gotha, where he penned some satirical verses on one of the masters, which brought him into some trouble. He removed in consequence to Weimar, where he pursued his classical studies under the direction of Franz Passow, at whose house he lodged. Unhappily, during his sojourn at Weimar his relations with his mother became strained. One feels that there is a sort of autobiographical interest in his essay on women, that his view was largely influenced by his relations with his mother, just as one feels that his particular argument in his essay on education is largely influenced by the course of his own training.

On his coming of age Schopenhauer was entitled to a share of the paternal estate, a share which yielded him a yearly income of about £150. He now entered himself at the University of Göttingen (October 1809), enrolling himself as a student of medicine, and devoting himself to the study of the natural sciences, mineralogy, anatomy, mathematics, and history; later, he included logic, physiology, and ethnography. He had always been passionately devoted to music and found relaxation in learning to play the flute and guitar. His studies at this time did not preoccupy him to the extent of isolation; he mixed freely with his fellows, and reckoned amongst his friends or acquaintances, F.W. Kreise, Bunsen, and Ernst Schulze. During one vacation he went on an expedition to Cassel and to the Hartz Mountains. It was about this time, and partly owing to the influence of Schulze, the author of *Aenesidemus*, and then a professor at the University of Göttingen, that Schopenhauer came to realise his vocation as that of a philosopher.

During his holiday at Weimar he called upon Wieland, then seventy-eight years old, who, probably prompted by Mrs. Schopenhauer, tried to dissuade him from the vocation which he had chosen. Schopenhauer in reply said, "Life is a difficult question; I have decided to spend my life in thinking about it." Then, after the conversation had continued for some little time, Wieland declared warmly that he thought that he had chosen rightly. "I understand your nature," he said; "keep to philosophy." And, later, he told Johanna Schopenhauer that he thought her son would be a great man some day.

Towards the close of the summer of 1811 Schopenhauer removed to Berlin and entered the University. He here continued his study of the natural sciences; he also attended the lectures on the History of Philosophy by Schleiermacher, and on Greek Literature and Antiquities by F.A. Wolf, and the lectures on "Facts of Consciousness" and "Theory of Science" by Fichte, for the last of whom, as we know indeed from frequent references in his books, he had no little contempt. A year or so later, when the news of Napoleon's disaster in Russia arrived, the Germans were thrown into a state of great excitement, and made speedy preparations for war. Schopenhauer contributed towards equipping volunteers for the army, but he did not enter active service; indeed, when the result of the battle of Lützen was known and Berlin seemed to be in danger, he fled for safety to Dresden and thence to Weimar. A little later we find him at Rudolstadt, whither he had proceeded in consequence of the recurrence of differences with his mother, and remained there from June to November 1813, principally engaged in the composition of an essay, "A Philosophical Treatise on the Fourfold Root of the Principle of Sufficient Reason," which he offered to the University of Jena as an exercise to qualify for the degree of Doctor of Philosophy, and for which a diploma was granted. He published this essay at his own cost towards the end of the year, but it seems to have fallen flatly from the press, although its arguments attracted the attention and the sympathy of Goethe, who, meeting him on his return to Weimar in November, discussed with him his own theory of colour. A couple of years before, Goethe, who was opposed to the Newtonian theory of light, had brought out his *Farbenlehre* (colour theory). In Goethe's diary Schopenhauer's name frequently occurs, and on the 24th November 1813 he wrote to Knebel: "Young Schopenhauer is a remarkable and interesting man.... I find him intellectual, but I am undecided about him as far as other things go." The result of this association with Goethe was his *Ueber das Sehn und die Farben* ("On Vision and Colour"), published at Leipzig in 1816, a copy of which he forwarded to Goethe (who had already seen the MS.) on the 4th May of that year. A few days later Goethe wrote to the distinguished scientist, Dr. Seebeck, asking him to read the work. In Gwinner's *Life* we find the copy of a letter written in English to Sir C.L. Eastlake: "In the year 1830, as I was going to publish in Latin the same treatise which in German accompanies this letter, I went to Dr. Seebeck of the Berlin Academy, who is universally admitted to be the first natural philosopher (in the English sense of the word meaning physiker) of Germany; he is the discoverer of thermo-electricity and of several physical truths. I questioned him on his opinion on the controversy between Goethe and Newton; he was extremely cautious and made me promise that I should not print and publish anything of what he might say, and at last, being hard pressed by me, he confessed that indeed Goethe was perfectly right and Newton wrong, but that he had no business to tell the world so. He has died since, the old coward!"

In May 1814 Schopenhauer removed from Weimar to Dresden, in consequence of the recurrence of domestic differences with his mother. This was the final break between the pair, and he did not see her again during the remaining twenty-four years of her life, although they resumed correspondence some years before her death. It were futile to attempt to revive the dead bones of the cause of these unfortunate differences between Johanna Schopenhauer and her son. It was a question of opposing temperaments; both and neither were at once to blame. There is no reason to suppose that Schopenhauer was ever a conciliatory son, or a companionable person to live with; in fact, there is plenty to show that he possessed trying and irritating qualities, and that he assumed an attitude of criticism towards his mother that could not in any circumstances be agreeable. On the other hand, Anselm Feuerbach in his *Memoirs* furnishes us with a scarcely prepossessing picture of Mrs. Schopenhauer: "Madame Schopenhauer," he writes, "a rich widow. Makes profession of erudition. Authoress. Prattles much and well, intelligently; without heart and soul. Self-complacent, eager after approbation, and constantly smiling to herself. God preserve us from women whose mind has shot up into mere intellect."

Schopenhauer meanwhile was working out his philosophical system, the idea of his principal philosophical work. "Under my hands," he wrote in 1813, "and still more in my mind grows a work, a philosophy which will be an ethics and a metaphysics in one: - two branches which hitherto have been separated as falsely as man has been divided into soul and body. The work grows, slowly and gradually aggregating its parts like the child in the womb. I became aware of one member, one vessel, one part after another. In other words, I set each sentence down without anxiety as to how it will fit into the whole; for I know it has all sprung from a single foundation. It is thus that an organic whole originates, and that alone will live.... Chance, thou ruler of this sense-world! Let me live and find peace for yet a few years, for I love my work as the mother her child. When it is matured and has come to birth, then exact from me thy duties, taking interest for the postponement. But, if I sink before the time in this iron age, then grant that these miniature beginnings, these studies of mine, be given to the world as they are and for what they are: some day perchance will arise a kindred spirit, who can frame the members together and 'restore' the fragment of antiquity."[1]

By March 1817 he had completed the preparatory work of his system, and began to put the whole thing together; a year later *Die Welt als Wille und Vorstellung: vier Bücher, nebst einem Anhange, der die Kritik der Kantischen Philosophie enthält* ("The World as Will and Idea; four books, with an appendix containing a criticism on the philosophy of Kant"). Some delay occurring in the publication, Schopenhauer wrote one of his characteristically abusive letters to Brockhaus, his publisher, who retorted "that he must decline all further correspondence with one whose letters, in their divine coarseness and rusticity, savoured more of the cabman than of the philosopher," and concluded with a hope that his fears that the work he was printing would be good for nothing but waste paper, might not be realised.[2] The work appeared about the end of December 1818 with 1819 on the title-page. Schopenhauer had meanwhile proceeded in September to Italy, where he revised the final proofs. So far as the reception of the work was concerned there was reason to believe that the fears of Brockhaus would be realised, as, in fact, they came practically to be. But in the face of this general want of appreciation, Schopenhauer had some crumbs of consolation. His sister wrote to him in March (he was then staying at Naples) that Goethe "had received it with great joy, immediately cut the thick book, and began *instantly* to read it. An hour later he sent me a note to say that he thanked you very much and thought that the whole book was good. He pointed out the most important passages, read them to us, and was greatly delighted.... You are the only author whom Goethe has ever read seriously, it seems to me, and I rejoice." Nevertheless the book did not sell. Sixteen years later Brockhaus informed Schopenhauer that a large number of copies had been sold at waste paper price, and that he had even then a few in stock. Still, during the years 1842-43, Schopenhauer was contemplating the issue of a second edition and making revisions for that purpose; when he had completed the work he took it to Brockhaus, and agreed to leave the question of remuneration open. In the following year the second edition was issued (500 copies of the first volume, and 750 of the second), and for this the author was to receive no remuneration. "Not to my contemporaries," says Schopenhauer with fine conviction in his preface to this edition, "not to my compatriots – to mankind I commit my now completed work, in the confidence that it will not be without value for them, even if this should be late recognised, as is commonly the lot of what is good. For it cannot have been for the passing generation, engrossed with the delusion of the moment, that my mind, almost against my will, has uninterruptedly stuck to its work through the course of a long life. And while the lapse of time has not been able to make me doubt the worth of my work, neither has the lack of sympathy; for I constantly saw the false and the bad, and finally the absurd and senseless, stand in universal admiration and honour, and I bethought myself that if it were not the case, those who are capable of recognising the genuine and right are so rare that we may look for them in vain for some twenty years, then those who are capable of producing it could not be so few that their works afterwards form an exception to the perishableness of earthly things; and thus would be lost the reviving prospect of posterity which every one who sets before himself a high aim requires to strengthen him."[3]

When Schopenhauer started for Italy Goethe had provided him with a letter of introduction to Lord Byron, who was then staying at Venice, but Schopenhauer never made use of the letter; he said that he hadn't the courage to present himself. "Do you know," he says in a letter, "three great pessimists were in Italy at the same time – Byron, Leopardi, and myself! And yet not one of us has made the acquaintance of the other." He remained in Italy until June 1819, when he proceeded to Milan, where he received distressing news from his sister to the effect that a Dantzic firm, in which she and her mother had invested all their capital, and in which he himself had invested a little, had become bankrupt. Schopenhauer immediately proposed to share his own income with them. But later, when the defaulting firm offered to its creditors a composition of thirty per cent, Schopenhauer would accept nothing less than seventy per cent in the case of immediate payment, or the whole if the payment were deferred; and he was so indignant at his mother and sister falling in with the arrangement of the debtors, that he did not correspond with them again for eleven years. With reference to this affair he wrote: "I can imagine that from your point of view my behaviour may seem hard and unfair. That is a mere illusion which disappears as soon as you reflect that all I want is merely not to have taken from me what is most rightly and incontestably mine, what, moreover, my whole happiness, my freedom, my learned leisure depend upon; - a blessing which in this world people like me enjoy so rarely that it would be almost as unconscientious as cowardly not to defend it to the uttermost and maintain it by every exertion. You say, perhaps, that if all your creditors were of this way of thinking, I too should come badly off. But if all men thought as I do, there would be much more thinking done, and in that case probably there would be neither bankruptcies, nor wars, nor gaming tables."[4]

In July 1819, when he was at Heidelberg, the idea occurred to him of turning university lecturer, and took practical shape the following summer, when he delivered a course of lectures on philosophy at the Berlin University. But the experiment was not a success; the course was not completed through the want of attendance, while Hegel at the same time and place was lecturing to a crowded and enthusiastic audience. This failure embittered him, and during the next few years there is little of any moment in his life to record. There was one incident, however, to which his detractors would seem to have attached more importance than it was worth, but which must have been sufficiently disturbing to

Schopenhauer – we refer to the Marquet affair. It appears on his returning home one day he found three women gossiping outside his door, one of whom was a seamstress who occupied another room in the house. Their presence irritated Schopenhauer (whose sensitiveness in such matters may be estimated from his essay "On Noise"), who, finding them occupying the same position on another occasion, requested them to go away, but the seamstress replied that she was an honest person and refused to move. Schopenhauer disappeared into his apartments and returned with a stick. According to his own account, he offered his arm to the woman in order to take her out; but she would not accept it, and remained where she was. He then threatened to put her out, and carried his threat into execution by seizing her round the waist and putting her out. She screamed, and attempted to return. Schopenhauer now pushed her out; the woman fell, and raised the whole house. This woman, Caroline Luise Marquet, brought an action against him for damages, alleging that he had kicked and beaten her. Schopenhauer defended his own case, with the result that the action was dismissed. The woman appealed, and Schopenhauer, who was contemplating going to Switzerland, did not alter his plans, so that the appeal was heard during his absence, the judgment reversed, and he was mulcted in a fine of twenty thalers. But the unfortunate business did not end here. Schopenhauer proceeded from Switzerland to Italy, and did not return to Berlin until May 1825. Caroline Marquet renewed her complaints before the courts, stating that his ill-usage had occasioned a fever through which she had lost the power of one of her arms, that her whole system was entirely shaken, and demanding a monthly allowance as compensation. She won her case; the defendant had to pay three hundred thalers in costs and contribute sixty thalers a year to her maintenance while she lived. Schopenhauer on returning to Berlin did what he could to get the judgment reversed, but unsuccessfully. The woman lived for twenty years; he inscribed on her death certificate, "*Obit anus, obit onus*"

The idea of marriage seems to have more or less possessed Schopenhauer about this time, but he could not finally determine to take the step. There is sufficient to show in the following essays in what light he regarded women. Marriage was a debt, he said, contracted in youth and paid off in old age. Married people have the whole burden of life to bear, while the unmarried have only half, was a characteristically selfish apothegm. Had not all the true philosophers been celibates - Descartes, Leibnitz, Malebranche, Spinoza, and Kant? The classic writers were of course not to be considered, because with them woman occupied a subordinate position. Had not all the great poets married, and with disastrous consequences? Plainly, Schopenhauer was not the person to sacrifice the individual to the will of the species.

In August 1831 he made a fortuitous expedition to Frankfort-on-the-Main - an expedition partly prompted by the outbreak of cholera at Berlin at the time, and partly by the portent of a dream (he was credulous in such matters) which at the beginning of the year had intimated his death. Here, however, he practically remained until his death, leading a quiet, mechanically regular life and devoting his thoughts to the development of his philosophic ideas, isolated at first, but as time went on enjoying somewhat greedily the success which had been denied him in his earlier days. In February 1839 he had a moment of elation when he heard from the Scientific Society of Drontheim that he had won the prize for the best essay on the question, "Whether free will could be proved from the evidence of consciousness," and that he had been elected a member of the Society; and a corresponding moment of despondency when he was informed by the Royal Danish Academy of the Sciences at Copenhagen, in a similar competition, that his essay on "Whether the source and foundation of ethics was to be sought in an intuitive moral idea, and in the analysis of other derivative moral conceptions, or in some other principle of knowledge," had failed, partly on the ground of the want of respect which it showed to the opinions of the chief philosophers. He published these essays in 1841 under the title of

"The Two Fundamental Problems of Ethics," and ten years later *Parerga und Paralipomena* the composition of which had engaged his attention for five or six years. The latter work, which proved to be his most popular, was refused by three publishers, and when eventually it was accepted by Hayn of Berlin, the author only received ten free copies of his work as payment. It is from this book that all except one of the following essays have been selected; the exception is "The Metaphysics of Love," which appears in the supplement of the third book of his principal work. The second edition of *Die Welt als Wille und Vorstellung* appeared in 1844, and was received with growing appreciation. Hitherto he had been chiefly known in Frankfort as the son of the celebrated Johanna Schopenhauer; now he came to have a following which, if at first small in numbers, were sufficiently enthusiastic, and proved, indeed, so far as his reputation was concerned, helpful. Artists painted his portrait; a bust of him was made by Elizabeth Ney. In the April number of the *Westminster Review* for 1853 John Oxenford, in an article entitled "Iconoclasm in German Philosophy," heralded in England his recognition as a writer and thinker; three years later Saint-René Taillandier, in the *Revue des Deux Mondes*, did a similar service for him in France. One of his most enthusiastic admirers was Richard Wagner, who in 1854 sent him a copy of his *Der Ring der Nibelungen*, with the inscription "In admiration and gratitude." The Philosophical Faculty of the University of Leipzic offered a prize for an exposition and criticism of his philosophical system. Two Frenchmen, M. Foucher de Careil and M. Challemel Lacour, who visited Schopenhauer during his last days, have given an account of their impressions of the interview, the latter in an article entitled, "Un Bouddhiste Contemporain en Allemagne," which appeared in the *Revue des Deux Mondes* for March 15th, 1870. M. Foucher de Careil gives a charming picture of him: – "Quand je le vis, pour la première fois, en 1859, à la table de l'hôtel d'Angleterre, à Francfort, c'était déjà un vieillard, à l'oeil d'un bleu vif et limpide, à la lèvre mince et légèrement sarcastique, autour de laquelle errait un fin sourire, et dont le vaste front, estompé de deux touffes de cheveux blancs sur les côtés, relevait d'un cachet de noblesse et de distinction la physionomie petillante d'esprit et de malice. Les habits, son jabot de dentelle, sa cravate blanche rappelaient un vieillard de la fin du règne de Louis XV; ses manières étaient celles d'un homme de bonne compagnie. Habituellement réservé et d'un naturel craintif jusqu'à la méfiance, il ne se livrait qu'avec ses intimes ou les étrangers de passage à Francfort. Ses mouvements étaient vifs et devenaient d'une pétulance extraordinaire dans la conversation; il fuyait les discussions et les vains combats de paroles, mais c'était pour mieux jouir du charme d'une causerie intime. Il possédait et parlait avec une égale perfection quatre langues: le français, l'anglais, l'allemand, l'italien et passablement l'espagnol. Quand il causait, la verve du vieillard brodait sur le canevas un peu lourd de l'allemand ses brilliantes arabesques latines, grecques, françaises, anglaises, italiennes. C'était un entrain, une précision et des sailles, une richesse de citations, une exactitude de détails qui faisait couler les heures; et quelquefois le petit cercle de ses intimes l'écoutait jusqu'à minuit, sans qu'un moment de fatigue se fût peint sur ses traits ou que le feu de son regard se fût un instant amorti. Sa parole nette et accentuée captivait l'auditoire: elle peignait et analysait tout ensemble; une sensibilité délicate en augmentait le feu; elle était exacte et précise sur toutes sortes de sujets."

Schopenhauer died on the 20th September 1860, in his seventy-third year, peacefully, alone as he had lived, but not without warning. One day in April, taking his usual brisk walk after dinner, he suffered from palpitation of the heart, he could scarcely breathe. These symptoms developed during the next few months, and Dr. Gwinner advised him to discontinue his cold baths and to breakfast in bed; but Schopenhauer, notwithstanding his early medical training, was little inclined to follow medical advice. To Dr. Gwinner, on the evening of the 18th September, when he expressed a hope that he might be able to go to Italy, he said that it would be a pity if he died now, as he wished to make several important additions to his *Parerga;* he spoke about his works and of the warm recognition with which they had been welcomed in the most remote places. Dr. Gwinner had never before found him so eager and gentle, and left him reluctantly, without, however, the least premonition that he had seen him for the last time. On the second morning after this interview Schopenhauer got up as usual, and had his cold bath and breakfast. His servant had opened the window to let in the morning air and had then left him. A little later Dr. Gwinner arrived and found him reclining in a corner of the sofa; his face wore its customary expression; there was no sign of there having been any struggle with death. There had been no struggle with death; he had died, as he had hoped he would die, painlessly, easily.

In preparing the above notice the writer has to acknowledge her indebtedness to Dr. Gwinner's *Life* and Professor Wallace's little work on the same subject, as well as to the few other authorities that have been available. – THE TRANSLATOR.

NOTES

1. Wallace's *Life*, pp. 95, 96.
2. Wallace, p. 108.
3. Haldane and Kemp's *The World as Will and Idea*.
4. Wallace, p. 145.

ON AUTHORSHIP

There are, first of all, two kinds of authors: those who write for the subject's sake, and those who write for writing's sake. While the one have had thoughts or experiences which seem to them worth communicating, the others want money; and so they write, for money. Their thinking is part of the business of writing. They may be recognized by the way in which they spin out their thoughts to the greatest possible length; then, too, by the very nature of their thoughts, which are only half-true, perverse, forced, vacillating; again, by the aversion they generally show to saying anything straight out, so that they may seem other than they are. Hence their writing is deficient in clearness and definiteness, and it is not long before they betray that their only object in writing at all is to cover paper. This sometimes happens with the best authors; now and then, for example, with Lessing in his *Dramaturgie*, and even in many of Jean Paul's romances. As soon as the reader perceives this, let him throw the book away; for time is precious. The truth is that when an author begins to write for the sake of covering paper, he is cheating the reader; because he writes under the pretext that he has something to say.

Writing for money and reservation of copyright are, at bottom, the ruin of literature. No one writes anything that is worth writing, unless he writes entirely for the sake of his subject. What an inestimable boon it would be, if in every branch of literature there were only a few books, but those excellent! This can never happen, as long as money is to be made by writing. It seems as though the money lay under a curse; for every author degenerates as soon as he begins to put pen to paper in any way for the sake of gain. The best works of the greatest men all come from the time when they had to write for nothing or for very little. And here, too, that Spanish proverb holds good, which declares that honor and money are not to be found in the same purse - *honora y provecho no caben en un saco.* The reason why Literature is in such a bad plight nowadays is simply and solely that people write books to make money. A man who is in want sits down and writes a book, and the public is stupid enough to buy it. The secondary effect of this is the ruin of language.

A great many bad writers make their whole living by that foolish mania of the public for reading nothing but what has just been printed, - journalists, I mean. Truly, a most appropriate name. In plain language it is *journeymen, day-laborers*!

Again, it may be said that there are three kinds of authors. First come those who write without thinking. They write from a full memory, from reminiscences; it may be, even straight out of other people's books. This class is the most numerous. Then come those who do their thinking whilst they are writing. They think in order to write; and there is no lack of them. Last of all come those authors who think before they begin to write. They are rare.

Authors of the second class, who put off their thinking until they come to write, are like a sportsman who goes forth at random and is not likely to bring very much home. On the other hand, when an author of the third or rare class writes, it is like a *battue.* Here the game has been previously captured and shut up within a very small space; from which it is afterwards let out, so many at a time, into another space, also confined. The game cannot possibly escape the sportsman; he has nothing to do but aim and fire - in other words, write down his thoughts. This is a kind of sport from which a man has something to show.

But even though the number of those who really think

seriously before they begin to write is small, extremely few of them think about *the subject itself*: the remainder think only about the books that have been written on the subject, and what has been said by others. In order to think at all, such writers need the more direct and powerful stimulus of having other people's thoughts before them. These become their immediate theme; and the result is that they are always under their influence, and so never, in any real sense of the word, are original. But the former are roused to thought by the subject itself, to which their thinking is thus immediately directed. This is the only class that produces writers of abiding fame.

It must, of course, be understood that I am speaking here of writers who treat of great subjects; not of writers on the art of making brandy.

Unless an author takes the material on which he writes out of his own head, that is to say, from his own observation, he is not worth reading. Book-manufacturers, compilers, the common run of history-writers, and many others of the same class, take their material immediately out of books; and the material goes straight to their finger-tips without even paying freight or undergoing examination as it passes through their heads, to say nothing of elaboration or revision. How very learned many a man would be if he knew everything that was in his own books! The consequence of this is that these writers talk in such a loose and vague manner, that the reader puzzles his brain in vain to understand what it is of which they are really thinking. They are thinking of nothing. It may now and then be the case that the book from which they copy has been composed exactly in the same way: so that writing of this sort is like a plaster cast of a cast; and in the end, the bare outline of the face, and that, too, hardly recognizable, is all that is left to your Antinous. Let compilations be read as seldom as possible. It is difficult to avoid them altogether; since compilations also include those text-books which contain in a small space the accumulated knowledge of centuries.

There is no greater mistake than to suppose that the last work is always the more correct; that what is written later on is in every case an improvement on what was written before; and that change always means progress. Real thinkers, men of right judgment, people who are in earnest with their subject, - these are all exceptions only. Vermin is the rule everywhere in the world: it is always on the alert, taking the mature opinions of the thinkers, and industriously seeking to improve upon them (save the mark!) in its own peculiar way.

If the reader wishes to study any subject, let him beware of rushing to the newest books upon it, and confining his attention to them alone, under the notion that science is always advancing, and that the old books have been drawn upon in the writing of the new. They have been drawn upon, it is true; but how? The writer of the new book often does not understand the old books thoroughly, and yet he is unwilling to take their exact words; so he bungles them, and says in his own bad way that which has been said very much better and more clearly by the old writers, who wrote from their own lively knowledge of the subject. The new writer frequently omits the best things they say, their most striking illustrations, their happiest remarks; because he does not see their value or feel how pregnant they are. The only thing that appeals to him is what is shallow and insipid.

It often happens that an old and excellent book is ousted by new and bad ones, which, written for money, appear with an air of great pretension and much puffing on the part of friends. In science a man tries to make his mark by bringing out something fresh. This often means nothing more than that he attacks some received theory which is quite correct, in order to make room for his own false notions. Sometimes the effort is successful for a time; and then a return is made to the old and true theory. These innovators are serious about nothing but their own precious self: it is this that they want to put forward, and the quick way of doing so, as they think, is to start a paradox. Their sterile heads take naturally to the path of negation; so they begin to deny truths that have long been admitted - the vital power, for example, the sympathetic nervous system, *generatio equivoca*, Bichat's distinction between the working of the passions and the working of intelligence; or else they want us to return to crass atomism, and the like. Hence it frequently happens that *the course of science is retrogressive.*

To this class of writers belong those translators who not only translate their author but also correct and revise him; a proceeding which always seems to me impertinent. To such writers I say: Write books yourself which are worth translating, and leave other people's works as they are!

The reader should study, if he can, the real authors, the men who have founded and discovered things; or, at any rate, those who are recognized as the great masters in every branch of knowledge. Let him buy second-hand books rather than read their contents in new ones. To be sure, it is easy to add to any new discovery – *inventis aliquid addere facile est;* and, therefore, the student, after well mastering the rudiments of his subject, will have to make himself acquainted with the more recent additions to the knowledge of it. And, in general, the following rule may be laid down here as elsewhere: if a thing is new, it is seldom good; because if it is good, it is only for a short time new.

What the address is to a letter, the title should be to a book; in other words, its main object should be to bring the book to those amongst the public who will take an interest in its contents. It should, therefore, be expressive; and since by its very nature it must be short, it should be concise, laconic, pregnant, and if possible give the contents in one word. A prolix title is bad; and so is one that says nothing, or is obscure and ambiguous, or even, it may be, false and misleading; this last may possibly involve the book in the same fate as overtakes a wrongly addressed letter. The worst titles of all are those which have been stolen, those, I mean, which have already been borne by other books; for they are in the first place a plagiarism, and secondly the most convincing proof of a total lack of originality in the author. A man who has not enough originality to invent a new title for his book, will be still less able to give it new contents. Akin to these stolen titles are those which have been imitated, that is to say, stolen to the extent of one half; for instance, long after I had produced my treatise *On Will in Nature*, Oersted wrote a book entitled *On Mind in Nature*.

A book can never be anything more than the impress of its author's thoughts; and the value of these will lie either in *the matter about which he has thought*, or in the *form* which his thoughts take, in other words, *what it is that he has thought about it.*

The matter of books is most various; and various also are the several excellences attaching to books on the score of their matter. By matter I mean everything that comes within the domain of actual experience; that is to say, the facts of history and the facts of nature, taken in and by themselves and in their widest sense. Here it is the *thing* treated of, which gives its peculiar character to the book; so that a book can be important, whoever it was that wrote it.

But in regard to the form, the peculiar character of a book depends upon the *person* who wrote it. It may treat of matters which are accessible to everyone and well known; but it is the way in which they are treated, what it is that is thought about them, that gives the book its value; and this comes from its author. If, then, from this point of view a book is excellent and beyond comparison, so is its author. It follows that if a writer is worth reading, his merit rises just in proportion as he owes little to his matter; therefore, the better known and the more hackneyed this is, the greater he will be. The three great tragedians of Greece, for example, all worked at the same subject-matter.

So when a book is celebrated, care should be taken to note whether it is so on account of its matter or its form; and a distinction should be made accordingly.

Books of great importance on account of their matter may proceed from very ordinary and shallow people, by the fact that they alone have had access to this matter; books, for instance, which describe journeys in distant lands, rare natural phenomena, or experiments; or historical occurrences of which the writers were witnesses, or in connection with which they have spent much time and trouble in the research and special study of original documents.

On the other hand, where the matter is accessible to everyone or very well known, everything will depend upon the form; and what it is that is thought about the matter will give the book all the value it possesses. Here only a really distinguished man will be able to produce anything worth reading; for the others will think nothing but what anyone else can think. They will just produce an impress of their own minds; but this is a print of which everyone possesses the original.

However, the public is very much more concerned to have matter than form; and for this very reason it is deficient in any high degree of culture. The public shows its preference in this respect in the most laughable way when it comes to deal with poetry; for there it devotes much trouble to the task of tracking out the actual events or personal circumstances in the life of the poet which served as the occasion of his various works; nay, these events and circumstances come in the end to be of greater importance than the works themselves; and rather than read Goethe himself, people prefer to read what has been written about him, and to study the legend of Faust more industriously than the drama of that name. And when Bürger declared that "people would write learned disquisitions on the question, Who Leonora really was," we find this literally fulfilled in Goethe's case; for we now possess a great many learned disquisitions on Faust and the legend attaching to him. Study of this kind is, and remains, devoted to the material of the drama alone. To give such preference to the matter over the form, is as though a man were to take a fine Etruscan vase, not to admire its shape or coloring, but to make a chemical analysis of the clay and paint of which it is composed.

The attempt to produce an effect by means of the material employed – an attempt which panders to this evil tendency of the public – is most to be condemned in branches of literature where any merit there may be lies expressly in the form; I mean, in poetical work. For all that, it is not rare to find bad dramatists trying to fill the house by means of the matter about which they write. For example, authors of this kind do not shrink from putting on the stage any man who is in any way celebrated, no matter whether his life may have been entirely devoid of dramatic incident; and sometimes, even, they do not wait until the persons immediately connected with him are dead.

The distinction between matter and form to which I am here alluding also holds good of conversation. The chief qualities which enable a man to converse well are intelligence, discernment, wit and vivacity: these supply the form of conversation. But it is not long before attention has to be paid to the matter of which he speaks; in other words, the subjects about which it is possible to converse with him – his knowledge. If this is very small, his conversation will not be worth anything, unless he possesses the above-named formal qualities in a very exceptional degree; for he will have nothing to talk about but those facts of life and nature which everybody knows. It will be just the opposite, however, if a man is deficient in these formal qualities, but has an amount of knowledge which lends value to what he says. This value will then depend entirely upon the matter of his conversation; for, as the Spanish proverb has it, *mas sabe el necio en su casa, que el sabio en la agena* – a fool knows more of his own business than a wise man does of others.

ON STYLE

Style is the physiognomy of the mind, and a safer index to character than the face. To imitate another man's style is like wearing a mask, which, be it never so fine, is not long in arousing disgust and abhorrence, because it is lifeless; so that even the ugliest living face is better. Hence those who write in Latin and copy the manner of ancient authors, may be said to speak through a mask; the reader, it is true, hears what they say, but he cannot observe their physiognomy too; he cannot see their *style*. With the Latin works of writers who think for themselves, the case is different, and their style is visible; writers, I mean, who have not condescended to any sort of imitation, such as Scotus Erigena, Petrarch, Bacon, Descartes, Spinoza, and many others. An affectation in style is like making grimaces. Further, the language in which a man writes is the physiognomy of the nation to which he belongs; and here there are many hard and fast differences, beginning from the language of the Greeks, down to that of the Caribbean islanders.

To form a provincial estimate of the value of a writer's productions, it is not directly necessary to know the subject on which he has thought, or what it is that he has said about it; that would imply a perusal of all his works. It will be enough, in the main, to know *how* he has thought. This, which means the essential temper or general quality of his mind, may be precisely determined by his style. A man's style shows the *formal* nature of all his thoughts – the formal nature which can never change, be the subject or the character of his thoughts what it may: it is, as it were, the dough out of which all the contents of his mind are kneaded. When Eulenspiegel was asked how long it would take to walk to the next village, he gave the seemingly incongruous answer: *Walk*. He wanted to find out by the man's pace the distance he would cover in a given time. In the same way, when I have read a few pages of an author, I know fairly well how far he can bring me.

Every mediocre writer tries to mask his own natural style, because in his heart he knows the truth of what I am saying. He is thus forced, at the outset, to give up any attempt at being frank or naïve – a privilege which is thereby reserved for superior minds, conscious of their own worth, and therefore sure of themselves. What I mean is that these everyday writers are absolutely unable to resolve upon writing just as they think; because they have a notion that, were they to do so, their work might possibly look very childish and simple. For all that, it would not be without its value. If they would only go honestly to work, and say, quite simply, the things they have really thought, and just as they have thought them, these writers would be readable and, within their own proper sphere, even instructive.

But instead of that, they try to make the reader believe that their thoughts have gone much further and deeper than is really the case. They say what they have to say in long sentences that wind about in a forced and unnatural way; they coin new words and write prolix periods which go round and round the thought and wrap it up in a sort of disguise. They tremble between the two separate aims of communicating what they want to say and of concealing it. Their object is to dress it up so that it may look learned or deep, in order to give people the impression that there is very much more in it than for the moment meets the eye. They either jot down their thoughts bit by bit, in short, ambiguous, and paradoxical sentences, which apparently mean much more than they say, – of this kind of writing Schelling's treatises on natural philosophy are a splendid instance; or else they hold forth with a deluge of words and the most intolerable diffusiveness, as though no end of fuss were necessary to make the reader understand the deep meaning of their sentences, whereas it is some quite simple if not actually trivial idea, – examples of which may be found in plenty in the popular works of Fichte, and the philosophical manuals of a hundred other miserable dunces not worth mentioning; or, again, they try to write in some particular style which they have been pleased to take up and think very grand, a style, for example, *par excellence* profound and scientific, where the reader is tormented to death by the narcotic effect of longspun periods without a single idea in them, – such as are furnished in a special measure by those most impudent of all mortals, the Hegelians [1]; or it may be that it is an intellectual style they have striven after, where it seems as though their object were to go crazy altogether; and so on in many other cases. All these endeavors to put off the *nascetur ridiculus mus* – to avoid showing the funny little creature that is born after such mighty throes – often make it difficult to know what it is that they really mean. And then, too, they write down words, nay, even whole sentences, without attaching any meaning to them themselves, but in the hope that someone else will get sense out of them.

And what is at the bottom of all this? Nothing but the untiring effort to sell words for thoughts; a mode of merchandise that is always trying to make fresh openings for itself, and by means of odd expressions, turns of phrase, and combinations of every sort, whether new or used in a new sense, to produce the appearence of intellect in order to make up for the very painfully felt lack of it.

It is amusing to see how writers with this object in view will attempt first one mannerism and then another, as though they were putting on the mask of intellect! This mask may possibly deceive the inexperienced for a while, until it is seen to be a dead thing, with no life in it at all; it is then laughed at and exchanged for another. Such an author will at one moment write in a dithyrambic vein, as though he were tipsy; at another, nay, on the very next page, he will be pompous, severe, profoundly learned and prolix, stumbling on in the most cumbrous way and chopping up everything very small; like the late Christian Wolf, only in a modern dress. Longest of all lasts the mask of unintelligibility; but this is only in Germany, whither it was introduced by Fichte, perfected by Schelling, and carried to its highest pitch in Hegel - always with the best results.

And yet nothing is easier than to write so that no one can understand; just as contrarily, nothing is more difficult than to express deep things in such a way that every one must necessarily grasp them. All the arts and tricks I have been mentioning are rendered superfluous if the author really has any brains; for that allows him to show himself as he is, and confirms to all time Horace's maxim that good sense is the source and origin of good style:

Scribendi recte sapere est et principium et fons.

But those authors I have named are like certain workers in metal, who try a hundred different compounds to take the place of gold - the only metal which can never have any substitute. Rather than do that, there is nothing against which a writer should be more upon his guard than the manifest endeavor to exhibit more intellect than he really has; because this makes the reader suspect that he possesses very little; since it is always the case that if a man affects anything, whatever it may be, it is just there that he is deficient.

That is why it is praise to an author to say that he is *naïve;* it means that he need not shrink from showing himself as he is. Generally speaking, to be *naïve* is to be attractive; while lack of naturalness is everywhere repulsive. As a matter of fact we find that every really great writer tries to express his thoughts as purely, clearly, definitely and shortly as possible. Simplicity has always been held to be a mark of truth; it is also a mark of genius. Style receives its beauty from the thought it expresses; but with sham-thinkers the thoughts are supposed to be fine because of the style. Style is nothing but the mere silhouette of thought; and an obscure or bad style means a dull or confused brain.

The first rule, then, for a good style is that *the author should have something to say*; nay, this is in itself almost all that is necessary. Ah, how much it means! The neglect of this rule is a fundamental trait in the philosophical writing, and, in fact, in all the reflective literature, of my country, more especially since Fichte. These writers all let it be seen that they want to appear as though they had something to say; whereas they have nothing to say. Writing of this kind was brought in by the pseudo-philosophers at the Universities, and now it is current everywhere, even among the first literary notabilities of the age. It is the mother of that strained and vague style, where there seem to be two or even more meanings in the sentence; also of that prolix and cumbrous manner of expression, called *le stile empesé*; again, of that mere waste of words which consists in pouring them out like a flood; finally, of that trick of concealing the direst poverty of thought under a farrago of never-ending chatter, which clacks away like a windmill and quite stupefies one – stuff which a man may read for hours together without getting hold of a single clearly expressed and definite idea.[2] However, people are easy-going, and they have formed the habit of reading page upon page of all sorts of such verbiage, without having any particular idea of what the author really means. They fancy it is all as it should be, and fail to discover that he is writing simply for writing's sake.

On the other hand, a good author, fertile in ideas, soon wins his reader's confidence that, when he writes, he has really and truly *something to say*; and this gives the intelligent reader patience to follow him with attention. Such an author, just because he really has something to say, will never fail to express himself in the simplest and most straightforward manner; because his object is to awake the very same thought in the reader that he has in himself, and no other. So he will be able to affirm with Boileau that his thoughts are everywhere open to the light of the day, and that his verse always says something, whether it says it well or ill:

> *Ma pensée au grand jour partout s'offre et s'expose, Et mon vers, bien ou mal, dit toujours quelque chose:*

while of the writers previously described it may be asserted, in the words of the same poet, that they talk much and never say anything at all - *quiparlant beaucoup ne disent jamais rien.*

Another characteristic of such writers is that they always avoid a positive assertion wherever they can possibly do so, in order to leave a loophole for escape in case of need. Hence they never fail to choose the more *abstract* way of expressing themselves; whereas intelligent people use the more *concrete*; because the latter brings things more within the range of actual demonstration, which is the source of all evidence.

There are many examples proving this preference for abstract expression; and a particularly ridiculous one is afforded by the use of the verb *to condition* in the sense of *to cause* or *to produce.* People say *to condition something* instead of *to cause it,* because being abstract and indefinite it says less; it affirms that *A* cannot happen without *B*, instead of that *A* is caused by *B*. A back door is always left open; and this suits people whose secret knowledge of their own incapacity inspires them with a perpetual terror of all positive assertion; while with other people it is merely the effect of that tendency by which everything that is stupid in literature or bad in life is immediately imitated - a fact proved in either case by the rapid way in which it spreads. The Englishman uses his own judgment in what he writes as well as in what he does; but there is no nation of which this eulogy is less true than of the Germans. The consequence of this state of things is that the word *cause* has of late almost disappeared from the language of literature, and people talk only of *condition*. The fact is worth mentioning because it is so characteristically ridiculous.

The very fact that these commonplace authors are never more than half-conscious when they write, would be enough to account for their dullness of mind and the tedious things they produce. I say they are only half-conscious, because they really do not themselves understand the meaning of the words they use: they take words ready-made and commit them to memory. Hence when they write, it is not so much words as whole phrases that they put together - *phrases banales*. This is the explanation of that palpable lack of clearly-expressed thought in what they say. The fact is that they do not possess the die to give this stamp to their writing; clear thought of their own is just what they have not got. And what do we find in its place? - a vague, enigmatical intermixture of words, current phrases, hackneyed terms, and fashionable expressions. The result is that the foggy stuff they write is like a page printed with very old type.

On the other hand, an intelligent author really speaks to us when he writes, and that is why he is able to rouse our interest and commune with us. It is the intelligent author alone who puts individual words together with a full consciousness of their meaning, and chooses them with deliberate design. Consequently, his discourse stands to that of the writer described above, much as a picture that has been really painted, to one that has been produced by the use of a stencil. In the one case, every word, every touch of the brush, has a special purpose; in the other, all is done mechanically. The same distinction may be observed in music. For just as Lichtenberg says that Garrick's soul seemed to be in every muscle in his body, so it is the omnipresence of intellect that always and everywhere characterizes the work of genius.

I have alluded to the tediousness which marks the works of these writers; and in this connection it is to be observed, generally, that tediousness is of two kinds; objective and subjective. A work is objectively tedious when it contains the defect in question; that is to say, when its author has no perfectly clear thought or knowledge to communicate. For if a man has any clear thought or knowledge in him, his aim will be to communicate it, and he will direct his energies to this end; so that the ideas he furnishes are everywhere clearly expressed. The result is that he is neither diffuse, nor unmeaning, nor confused, and consequently not tedious. In such a case, even though the author is at bottom in error, the error is at any rate clearly worked out and well thought over, so that it is at least formally correct; and thus some value always attaches to the work. But for the same reason a work that is objectively tedious is at all times devoid of any value whatever.

The other kind of tediousness is only relative: a reader may find a work dull because he has no interest in the question treated of in it, and this means that his intellect is restricted. The best work may, therefore, be tedious subjectively, tedious, I mean, to this or that particular person; just as, contrarity, the worst work may be subjectively engrossing to this or that particular person who has an interest in the question treated of, or in the writer of the book.

It would generally serve writers in good stead if they would see that, whilst a man should, if possible, think like a great genius, he should talk the same language as everyone else. Authors should use common words to say uncommon things. But they do just the opposite. We find them trying to wrap up trivial ideas in grand words, and to clothe their very ordinary thoughts in the most extraordinary phrases, the most far-fetched, unnatural, and out-of-the-way expressions. Their sentences perpetually stalk about on stilts. They take so much pleasure in bombast, and write in such a high-flown, bloated, affected, hyperbolical and acrobatic style that their prototype is Ancient Pistol, whom his friend Falstaff once impatiently told to say what he had to say *like a man of this world.* [3]

There is no expression in any other language exactly answering to the French *stile empesé*; but the thing itself exists all the more often. When associated with affectation, it is in literature what assumption of dignity, grand airs and primeness are in society; and equally intolerable. Dullness of mind is fond of donning this dress; just as an ordinary life it is stupid people who like being demure and formal.

An author who writes in the prim style resembles a man who dresses himself up in order to avoid being confounded or put on the same level with a mob – a risk never run by the *gentleman*, even in his worst clothes. The plebeian may be known by a certain showiness of attire and a wish to have everything spick and span; and in the same way, the commonplace person is betrayed by his style.

Nevertheless, an author follows a false aim if he tries to write exactly as he speaks. There is no style of writing but should have a certain trace of kinship with the *epigraphic* or *monumental* style, which is, indeed, the ancestor of all styles. For an author to write as he speaks is just as reprehensible as the opposite fault, to speak as he writes; for this gives a pedantic effect to what he says, and at the same time makes him hardly intelligible.

An obscure and vague manner of expression is always and everywhere a very bad sign. In ninety-nine cases out of a hundred it comes from vagueness of thought; and this again almost always means that there is something radically wrong and incongruous about the thought itself – in a word, that it is incorrect. When a right thought springs up in the mind, it strives after expression and is not long in reaching it; for clear thought easily finds words to fit it. If a man is capable of thinking anything at all, he is also always able to express it in clear, intelligible, and unambiguous terms. Those writers who construct difficult, obscure, involved, and equivocal sentences, most certainly do not know aright what it is that they want to say: they have only a dull consciousness of it, which is still in the stage of struggle to shape itself as thought. Often, indeed, their desire is to conceal from themselves and others that they really have nothing at all to say. They wish to appear to know what they do not know, to think what they do not think, to say what they do not say. If a man has some real communication to make, which will he choose – an indistinct or a clear way of expressing himself? Even Quintilian remarks that things which are said by a highly educated man are often easier to understand and much clearer; and that the less educated a man is, the more obscurely he will write – *plerumque accidit ut faciliora sint ad intelligendum et lucidiora multo que a doctissimo quoque dicuntur.... Erit ergo etiam obscurior quo quisque deterior.*

An author should avoid enigmatical phrases; he should know whether he wants to say a thing or does not want to say it. It is this indecision of style that makes so many writers insipid. The only case that offers an exception to this rule arises when it is necessary to make a remark that is in some way improper.

As exaggeration generally produces an effect the opposite of that aimed at; so words, it is true, serve to make thought intelligible – but only up to a certain point. If words are heaped up beyond it, the thought becomes more and more obscure again. To find where the point lies is the problem of style, and the business of the critical faculty; for a word too much always defeats its purpose. This is what Voltaire means when he says that *the adjective is the enemy of the substantive*. But, as we have seen, many people try to conceal their poverty of thought under a flood of verbiage.

Accordingly let all redundancy be avoided, all stringing together of remarks which have no meaning and are not worth perusal. A writer must make a sparing use of the reader's time, patience and attention; so as to lead him to believe that his author writes what is worth careful study, and will reward the time spent upon it. It is always better to omit something good than to add that which is not worth saying at all. This is the right application of Hesiod's maxim, [Greek: pleon aemisu pantos] [4] – the half is more than the whole. *Le secret pour être ennuyeux, c'est de tout dire.* Therefore, if possible, the quintessence only! mere leading thoughts! nothing that the reader would think for himself. To use many words to communicate few thoughts is everywhere the unmistakable sign of mediocrity. To gather much thought into few words stamps the man of genius.

Truth is most beautiful undraped; and the impression it makes is deep in proportion as its expression has been simple. This is so, partly because it then takes unobstructed possession of the hearer's whole soul, and leaves him no by-thought to distract him; partly, also, because he feels that here he is not being corrupted or cheated by the arts of rhetoric, but that all the effect of what is said comes from the thing itself. For instance, what declamation on the vanity of human existence could ever be more telling than the words of Job? *Man that is born of a woman hath but a short time to live and is full of misery. He cometh up, and is cut down, like a flower; he fleeth as it were a shadow, and never continueth in one stay.*

For the same reason Goethe's naïve poetry is incomparably greater than Schiller's rhetoric. It is this, again, that makes many popular songs so affecting. As in architecture an excess of decoration is to be avoided, so in the art of literature a writer must guard against all rhetorical finery, all useless amplification, and all superfluity of expression in general; in a word, he must strive after *chastity* of style. Every word that can be spared is hurtful if it remains. The law of simplicity and naïveté holds good of all fine art; for it is quite possible to be at once simple and sublime.

True brevity of expression consists in everywhere saying only what is worth saying, and in avoiding tedious detail about things which everyone can supply for himself. This involves correct discrimination between what it necessary and what is superfluous. A writer should never be brief at the expense of being clear, to say nothing of being grammatical. It shows lamentable want of judgment to weaken the expression of a thought, or to stunt the meaning of a period for the sake of using a few words less. But this is the precise endeavor of that false brevity nowadays so much in vogue, which proceeds by leaving out useful words and even by sacrificing grammar and logic. It is not only that such writers spare a word by making a single verb or adjective do duty for several different periods, so that the reader, as it were, has to grope his way through them in the dark; they also practice, in many other respects, an unseemingly economy of speech, in the effort to effect what they foolishly take to be brevity of expression and conciseness of style. By omitting something that might have thrown a light over the whole sentence, they turn it into a conundrum, which the reader tries to solve by going over it again and again.[5]

It is wealth and weight of thought, and nothing else, that gives brevity to style, and makes it concise and pregnant. If a writer's ideas are important, luminous, and generally worth communicating, they will necessarily furnish matter and substance enough to fill out the periods which give them expression, and make these in all their parts both grammatically and verbally complete; and so much will this be the case that no one will ever find them hollow, empty or feeble. The diction will everywhere be brief and pregnant, and allow the thought to find intelligible and easy expression, and even unfold and move about with grace.

Therefore instead of contracting his words and forms of speech, let a writer enlarge his thoughts. If a man has been thinned by illness and finds his clothes too big, it is not by cutting them down, but by recovering his usual bodily condition, that he ought to make them fit him again.

Let me here mention an error of style, very prevalent nowadays, and, in the degraded state of literature and the neglect of ancient languages, always on the increase; I mean *subjectivity*. A writer commits this error when he thinks it enough if he himself knows what he means and wants to say, and takes no thought for the reader, who is left to get at the bottom of it as best he can. This is as though the author were holding a monologue; whereas, it ought to be a dialogue; and a dialogue, too, in which he must express himself all the more clearly inasmuch as he cannot hear the questions of his interlocutor.

Style should for this very reason never be subjective, but

objective; and it will not be objective unless the words are so set down that they directly force the reader to think precisely the same thing as the author thought when he wrote them. Nor will this result be obtained unless the author has always been careful to remember that thought so far follows the law of gravity that it travels from head to paper much more easily than from paper to head; so that he must assist the latter passage by every means in his power. If he does this, a writer's words will have a purely objective effect, like that of a finished picture in oils; whilst the subjective style is not much more certain in its working than spots on the wall, which look like figures only to one whose phantasy has been accidentally aroused by them; other people see nothing but spots and blurs. The difference in question applies to literary method as a whole; but it is often established also in particular instances. For example, in a recently published work I found the following sentence: *I have not written in order to increase the number of existing books.* This means just the opposite of what the writer wanted to say, and is nonsense as well.

He who writes carelessly confesses thereby at the very outset that he does not attach much importance to his own thoughts. For it is only where a man is convinced of the truth and importance of his thoughts, that he feels the enthusiasm necessary for an untiring and assiduous effort to find the clearest, finest, and strongest expression for them, – just as for sacred relics or priceless works of art there are provided silvern or golden receptacles. It was this feeling that led ancient authors, whose thoughts, expressed in their own words, have lived thousands of years, and therefore bear the honored title of *classics*, always to write with care. Plato, indeed, is said to have written the introduction to his *Republic* seven times over in different ways.[6]

As neglect of dress betrays want of respect for the company a man meets, so a hasty, careless, bad style shows an outrageous lack of regard for the reader, who then rightly punishes it by refusing to read the book. It is especially amusing to see reviewers criticising the works of others in their own most careless style – the style of a hireling. It is as though a judge were to come into court in dressing-gown and slippers! If I see a man badly and dirtily dressed, I feel some hesitation, at first, in entering into conversation with him: and when, on taking up a book, I am struck at once by the negligence of its style, I put it away.

Good writing should be governed by the rule that a man can think only one thing clearly at a time; and, therefore, that he should not be expected to think two or even more things in one and the same moment. But this is what is done when a writer breaks up his principal sentence into little pieces, for the purpose of pushing into the gaps thus made two or three other thoughts by way of parenthesis; thereby unnecessarily and wantonly confusing the reader. And here it is again my own countrymen who are chiefly in fault. That German lends itself to this way of writing, makes the thing possible, but does not justify it. No prose reads more easily or pleasantly than French, because, as a rule, it is free from the error in question. The Frenchman strings his thoughts together, as far as he can, in the most logical and natural order, and so lays them before his reader one after the other for convenient deliberation, so that every one of them may receive undivided attention. The German, on the other hand, weaves them together into a sentence which he twists and crosses, and crosses and twists again; because he wants to say six things all at once, instead of advancing them one by one. His aim should be to attract and hold the reader's attention; but, above and beyond neglect of this aim, he demands from the reader that he shall set the above mentioned rule at defiance, and think three or four different thoughts at one and the same time; or since that is impossible, that his thoughts shall succeed each other as quickly as the vibrations of a cord. In this way an author lays the foundation of his *stile empesé,* which is then carried to perfection by the use of high-flown, pompous expressions to communicate the simplest things, and other artifices of the same kind.

In those long sentences rich in involved parenthesis, like a box of boxes one within another, and padded out like roast geese stuffed with apples, it is really the *memory* that is chiefly taxed; while it is the understanding and the judgment which should be called into play, instead of having their activity thereby actually hindered and weakened.[7] This kind of sentence furnishes the reader with mere half-phrases, which he is then called upon to collect carefully and store up in his memory, as though they were the pieces of a torn letter, afterwards to be completed and made sense of by the other halves to which they respectively belong. He is expected to go on reading for a little without exercising any thought, nay, exerting only his memory, in the hope that, when he comes to the end of the sentence, he may see its meaning and so receive something to think about; and he is thus given a great deal to learn by heart before obtaining anything to understand. This is manifestly wrong and an abuse of the reader's patience.

The ordinary writer has an unmistakable preference for this style, because it causes the reader to spend time and trouble in understanding that which he would have understood in a moment without it; and this makes it look as though the writer had more depth and intelligence than the reader. This is, indeed, one of those artifices referred to above, by means of which mediocre authors unconsciously, and as it were by instinct, strive to conceal their poverty of thought and give an appearance of the opposite. Their ingenuity in this respect is really astounding.

It is manifestly against all sound reason to put one thought obliquely on top of another, as though both together formed a wooden cross. But this is what is done where a writer interrupts what he has begun to say, for the purpose of inserting some quite alien matter; thus depositing with the reader a meaningless half-sentence, and bidding him keep it until the completion comes. It is much as though a man were to treat his guests by handing them an empty plate, in the hope of something appearing upon it. And commas used for a similar purpose belong to the same family as notes at the foot of the page and parenthesis in the middle of the text; nay, all three differ only in degree. If Demosthenes and Cicero occasionally inserted words by ways of parenthesis, they would have done better to have refrained.

But this style of writing becomes the height of absurdity when the parenthesis are not even fitted into the frame of the sentence, but wedged in so as directly to shatter it. If, for instance, it is an impertinent thing to interrupt another person when he is speaking, it is no less impertinent to interrupt oneself. But all bad, careless, and hasty authors, who scribble with the bread actually before their eyes, use this style of writing six times on a page, and rejoice in it. It consists in – it is advisable to give rule and example together, wherever it is possible – breaking up one phrase in order to glue in another. Nor is it merely out of laziness that they write thus. They do it out of stupidity; they think there is a charming *légèreté* about it; that it gives life to what they say. No doubt there are a few rare cases where such a form of sentence may be pardonable.

Few write in the way in which an architect builds; who, before he sets to work, sketches out his plan, and thinks it over down to its smallest details. Nay, most people write only as though they were playing dominoes; and, as in this game, the pieces are arranged half by design, half by chance, so it is with the sequence and connection of their sentences. They only have an idea of what the general shape of their work will be, and of the aim they set before themselves. Many are ignorant even of this, and write as the coral-insects build; period joins to period, and the Lord only knows what the author means.

Life now-a-days goes at a gallop; and the way in which this affects literature is to make it extremely superficial and slovenly.

NOTES

1. In their Hegel-gazette, commonly known as *Jahrbücher der wissenschaftlichen Literatur*.
2. Select examples of the art of writing in this style are to be found almost *passim* in the *Jahrbücher* published at Halle, afterwards called the *Deutschen Jahrbücher*.
3. *King Henry IV.*, Part II. Act v. Sc. 3.
4. *Works and Days*, 40.
5. *Translator's Note.* – In the original, Schopenhauer here enters upon a lengthy examination of certain common errors in the writing and speaking of German. His remarks are addressed to his own countrymen, and would lose all point, even if they were intelligible, in an English translation. But for those who practice their German by conversing or corresponding with Germans, let me recommend what he there says as a useful corrective to a slipshod style, such as can easily be contracted if it is assumed that the natives of a country always know their own language perfectly.
6. *Translator's Note.* – It is a fact worth mentioning that the first twelve words of the *Republic* are placed in the exact order which would be natural in English.
7. *Translator's Note.* – This sentence in the original is obviously meant to illustrate the fault of which it speaks. It does so by the use of a construction very common in German, but happily unknown in English; where, however, the fault itself exists none the less, though in different form.

ON THE STUDY OF LATIN

The abolition of Latin as the universal language of learned men, together with the rise of that provincialism which attaches to national literatures, has been a real misfortune for the cause of knowledge in Europe. For it was chiefly through the medium of the Latin language that a learned public existed in Europe at all – a public to which every book as it came out directly appealed. The number of minds in the whole of Europe that are capable of thinking and judging is small, as it is; but when the audience is broken up and severed by differences of language, the good these minds can do is very much weakened. This is a great disadvantage; but a second and worse one will follow, namely, that the ancient languages will cease to be taught at all. The neglect of them is rapidly gaining ground both in France and Germany.

If it should really come to this, then farewell, humanity! farewell, noble taste and high thinking! The age of barbarism will return, in spite of railways, telegraphs and balloons. We shall thus in the end lose one more advantage possessed by all our ancestors. For Latin is not only a key to the knowledge of Roman antiquity; its also directly opens up to us the Middle Age in every country in Europe, and modern times as well, down to about the year 1750. Erigena, for example, in the ninth century, John of Salisbury in the twelfth, Raimond Lully in the thirteenth, with a hundred others, speak straight to us in the very language that they naturally adopted in thinking of learned matters.

They thus come quite close to us even at this distance of time: we are in direct contact with them, and really come to know them. How would it have been if every one of them spoke in the language that was peculiar to his time and country? We should not understand even the half of what they said. A real intellectual contact with them would be impossible. We should see them like shadows on the farthest horizon, or, may be, through the translator's telescope.

It was with an eye to the advantage of writing in Latin that Bacon, as he himself expressly states, proceeded to translate his *Essays* into that language, under the title *Sermones fideles*; at which work Hobbes assisted him.[1]

Here let me observe, by way of parenthesis, that when patriotism tries to urge its claims in the domain of knowledge, it commits an offence which should not be tolerated. For in those purely human questions which interest all men alike, where truth, insight, beauty, should be of sole account, what can be more impertinent than to let preference for the nation to which a man's precious self happens to belong, affect the balance of judgment, and thus supply a reason for doing violence to truth and being unjust to the great minds of a foreign country in order to make much of the smaller minds of one's own! Still, there are writers in every nation in Europe, who afford examples of this vulgar feeling. It is this which led Yriarte to caricature them in the thirty-third of his charming *Literary Fables*.[2]

In learning a language, the chief difficulty consists in making acquaintance with every idea which it expresses, even though it should use words for which there is no exact equivalent in the mother tongue; and this often happens. In learning a new language a man has, as it were, to mark out in his mind the boundaries of quite new spheres of ideas, with the result that spheres of ideas arise where none were before. Thus he not only learns words, he gains ideas too.

This is nowhere so much the case as in learning ancient languages, for the differences they present in their mode of expression as compared with modern languages is greater than can be found amongst modern languages as compared with one another. This is shown by the fact that in translating into Latin, recourse must be had to quite other turns of phrase than are used in the original. The thought that is to be translated has to be melted down and recast; in other words, it must be analyzed and then recomposed. It is just this process which makes the study of the ancient languages contribute so much to the education of the mind.

It follows from this that a man's thought varies according to the language in which he speaks. His ideas undergo a fresh modification, a different shading, as it were, in the study of every new language. Hence an acquaintance with many languages is not only of much indirect advantage, but it is also a direct means of mental culture, in that it corrects and matures ideas by giving prominence to their many-sided nature and their different varieties of meaning, as also that it increases dexterity of thought; for in the process of learning many languages, ideas become more and more independent of words. The ancient languages effect this to a greater degree than the modern, in virtue of the difference to which I have alluded.

From what I have said, it is obvious that to imitate the style of the ancients in their own language, which is so very much superior to ours in point of grammatical perfection, is the best way of preparing for a skillful and finished expression of thought in the mother-tongue. Nay, if a man wants to be a great writer, he must not omit to do this: just as, in the case of sculpture or painting, the student must educate himself by copying the great masterpieces of the past, before proceeding to original work. It is only by learning to write Latin that a man comes to treat diction as an art. The material in this art is language, which must therefore be handled with the greatest care and delicacy.

The result of such study is that a writer will pay keen

attention to the meaning and value of words, their order and connection, their grammatical forms. He will learn how to weigh them with precision, and so become an expert in the use of that precious instrument which is meant not only to express valuable thought, but to preserve it as well. Further, he will learn to feel respect for the language in which he writes and thus be saved from any attempt to remodel it by arbitrary and capricious treatment. Without this schooling, a man's writing may easily degenerate into mere chatter.

To be entirely ignorant of the Latin language is like being in a fine country on a misty day. The horizon is extremely limited. Nothing can be seen clearly except that which is quite close; a few steps beyond, everything is buried in obscurity. But the Latinist has a wide view, embracing modern times, the Middle Age and Antiquity; and his mental horizon is still further enlarged if he studies Greek or even Sanscrit.

If a man knows no Latin, he belongs to the vulgar, even though he be a great virtuoso on the electrical machine and have the base of hydrofluoric acid in his crucible.

There is no better recreation for the mind than the study of the ancient classics. Take any one of them into your hand, be it only for half an hour, and you will feel yourself refreshed, relieved, purified, ennobled, strengthened; just as though you had quenched your thirst at some pure spring. Is this the effect of the old language and its perfect expression, or is it the greatness of the minds whose works remain unharmed and unweakened by the lapse of a thousand years? Perhaps both together. But this I know. If the threatened calamity should ever come, and the ancient languages cease to be taught, a new literature will arise, of such barbarous, shallow and worthless stuff as never was seen before.

NOTES

1. Cf. Thomae Hobbes vita: *Carolopoli apud Eleutherium Anglicum*, 1681, p. 22.

2. *Translator's Note.* – Tomas de Yriarte (1750-91), a Spanish poet, and keeper of archives in the War Office at Madrid. His two best known works are a didactic poem, entitled *La Musica*, and the *Fables* here quoted, which satirize the peculiar foibles of literary men. They have been translated into many languages; into English by Rockliffe (3rd edition, 1866). The fable in question describes how, at a picnic of the animals, a discussion arose as to which of them carried off the palm for superiority of talent. The praises of the ant, the dog, the bee, and the parrot were sung in turn; but at last the ostrich stood up and declared for the dromedary. Whereupon the dromedary stood up and declared for the ostrich. No one could discover the reason for this mutual compliment. Was it because both were such uncouth beasts, or had such long necks, or were neither of them particularly clever or beautiful? or was it because each had a hump? *No!* said the fox, *you are all wrong. Don't you see they are both foreigners*? Cannot the same be said of many men of learning?

ON MEN OF LEARNING

When one sees the number and variety of institutions which exist for the purposes of education, and the vast throng of scholars and masters, one might fancy the human race to be very much concerned about truth and wisdom. But here, too, appearances are deceptive. The masters teach in order to gain money, and strive, not after wisdom, but the outward show and reputation of it; and the scholars learn, not for the sake of knowledge and insight, but to be able to chatter and give themselves airs. Every thirty years a new race comes into the world - a youngster that knows nothing about anything, and after summarily devouring in all haste the results of human knowledge as they have been accumulated for thousands of years, aspires to be thought cleverer than the whole of the past. For this purpose he goes to the University, and takes to reading books - new books, as being of his own age and standing. Everything he reads must be briefly put, must be new! he is new himself. Then he falls to and criticises. And here I am not taking the slightest account of studies pursued for the sole object of making a living.

Students, and learned persons of all sorts and every age, aim as a rule at acquiring *information* rather than insight. They pique themselves upon knowing about everything - stones, plants, battles, experiments, and all the books in existence. It never occurs to them that information is only a means of insight, and in itself of little or no value; that it is his way of *thinking* that makes a man a philosopher. When I hear of these portents of learning and their imposing erudition, I sometimes say to myself: Ah, how little they must have had to think about, to have been able to read so much! And when I actually find it reported of the elder Pliny that he was continually reading or being read to, at table, on a journey, or in his bath, the question forces itself upon my mind, whether the man was so very lacking in thought of his own that he had to have alien thought incessantly instilled into him; as though he were a consumptive patient taking jellies to keep himself alive. And neither his undiscerning credulity nor his inexpressibly repulsive and barely intelligible style - which seems like of a man taking notes, and very economical of paper - is of a kind to give me a high opinion of his power of independent thought.

We have seen that much reading and learning is prejudicial to thinking for oneself; and, in the same way, through much writing and teaching, a man loses the habit of being quite clear, and therefore thorough, in regard to the things he knows and understands; simply because he has left himself no time to acquire clearness or thoroughness. And so, when clear knowledge fails him in his utterances, he is forced to fill out the gaps with words and phrases. It is this, and not the dryness of the subject-matter, that makes most books such tedious reading. There is a saying that a good cook can make a palatable dish even out of an old shoe; and a good writer can make the dryest things interesting.

With by far the largest number of learned men, knowledge is a means, not an end. That is why they will never achieve any great work; because, to do that, he who pursues knowledge must pursue it as an end, and treat everything else, even existence itself, as only a means. For everything which a man fails to pursue for its own sake is but half-pursued; and true excellence, no matter in what sphere, can be attained only where the work has been produced for its own sake alone, and not as a means to further ends.

And so, too, no one will ever succeed in doing anything really great and original in the way of thought, who does not seek to acquire knowledge for himself, and, making this the immediate object of his studies, decline to trouble himself about the knowledge of others. But the average man of learning studies for the purpose of being able to teach and write. His head is like a stomach and intestines which let the food pass through them undigested. That is just why his teaching and writing is of so little use. For it is not upon undigested refuse that people can be nourished, but solely upon the milk which secretes from the very blood itself.

The wig is the appropriate symbol of the man of learning, pure and simple. It adorns the head with a copious quantity of false hair, in lack of one's own: just as erudition means endowing it with a great mass of alien thought. This, to be sure, does not clothe the head so well and naturally, nor is it so generally useful, nor so suited for all purposes, nor so firmly rooted; nor when alien thought is used up, can it be immediately replaced by more from the same source, as is the case with that which springs from soil of one's own. So we find Sterne, in his *Tristram Shandy*, boldly asserting that *an ounce of a man's own wit is worth a ton of other people's*.

And in fact the most profound erudition is no more akin to genius than a collection of dried plants in like Nature, with its constant flow of new life, ever fresh, ever young, ever changing. There are no two things more opposed than the childish naïveté of an ancient author and the learning of his commentator.

Dilettanti, dilettanti! This is the slighting way in which those who pursue any branch of art or learning for the love and enjoyment of the thing, – *per il loro diletto*, are spoken of by those who have taken it up for the sake of gain, attracted solely by the prospect of money. This contempt of theirs comes from the base belief that no man will seriously devote himself to a subject, unless he is spurred on to it by want, hunger, or else some form of greed. The public is of the same way of thinking; and hence its general respect for professionals and its distrust of *dilettanti.* But the truth is that the *dilettante* treats his subject as an end, whereas the professional, pure and simple, treats it merely as a means. He alone will be really in earnest about a matter, who has a direct interest therein, takes to it because he likes it, and pursues it *con amore.* It is these, and not hirelings, that have always done the greatest work.

In the republic of letters it is as in other republics; favor is shown to the plain man - he who goes his way in silence and does not set up to be cleverer than others. But the abnormal man is looked upon as threatening danger; people band together against him, and have, oh! such a majority on their side.

The condition of this republic is much like that of a small State in America, where every man is intent only upon his own advantage, and seeks reputation and power for himself, quite heedless of the general weal, which then goes to ruin. So it is in the republic of letters; it is himself, and himself alone, that a man puts forward, because he wants to gain fame. The only thing in which all agree is in trying to keep down a really eminent man, if he should chance to show himself, as one who would be a common peril. From this it is easy to see how it fares with knowledge as a whole.

Between professors and independent men of learning there has always been from of old a certain antagonism, which may perhaps be likened to that existing been dogs and wolves. In virtue of their position, professors enjoy great facilities for becoming known to their contemporaries. Contrarily, independent men of learning enjoy, by their position, great facilities for becoming known to posterity; to which it is necessary that, amongst other and much rarer gifts, a man should have a certain leisure and freedom. As mankind takes a long time in finding out on whom to bestow its attention, they may both work together side by side.

He who holds a professorship may be said to receive his food in the stall; and this is the best way with ruminant animals. But he who finds his food for himself at the hands of Nature is better off in the open field.

Of human knowledge as a whole and in every branch of it, by far the largest part exists nowhere but on paper, – I mean, in books, that paper memory of mankind. Only a small part of it is at any given period really active in the minds of particular persons. This is due, in the main, to the brevity and uncertainty of life; but it also comes from the fact that men are lazy and bent on pleasure. Every generation attains, on its hasty passage through existence, just so much of human knowledge as it needs, and then soon disappears. Most men of learning are very superficial. Then follows a new generation, full of hope, but ignorant, and with everything to learn from the beginning. It seizes, in its turn, just so much as it can grasp or find useful on its brief journey and then too goes its way. How badly it would fare with human knowledge if it were not for the art of writing and printing! This it is that makes libraries the only sure and lasting memory of the human race, for its individual members have all of them but a very limited and imperfect one. Hence most men of learning as are loth to have their knowledge examined as merchants to lay bare their books.

Human knowledge extends on all sides farther than the eye can reach; and of that which would be generally worth knowing, no one man can possess even the thousandth part.

All branches of learning have thus been so much enlarged that he who would "do something" has to pursue no more than one subject and disregard all others. In his own subject he will then, it is true, be superior to the vulgar; but in all else he will belong to it. If we add to this that neglect of the ancient languages, which is now-a-days on the increase and is doing away with all general education in the humanities – for a mere smattering of Latin and Greek is of no use – we shall come to have men of learning who outside their own subject display an ignorance truly bovine.

An exclusive specialist of this kind stands on a par with a workman in a factory, whose whole life is spent in making one particular kind of screw, or catch, or handle, for some particular instrument or machine, in which, indeed, he attains incredible dexterity. The specialist may also be likened to a man who lives in his own house and never leaves it. There he is perfectly familiar with everything, every little step, corner, or board; much as Quasimodo in Victor Hugo's *Nôtre Dame* knows the cathedral; but outside it, all is strange and unknown.

For true culture in the humanities it is absolutely necessary that a man should be many-sided and take large views; and for a man of learning in the higher sense of the word, an extensive acquaintance with history is needful. He, however, who wishes to be a complete philosopher, must gather into his head the remotest ends of human knowledge: for where else could they ever come together?

It is precisely minds of the first order that will never be specialists. For their very nature is to make the whole of existence their problem; and this is a subject upon which they will every one of them in some form provide mankind with a new revelation. For he alone can deserve the name of genius who takes the All, the Essential, the Universal, for the theme of his achievements; not he who spends his life in explaining some special relation of things one to another.

ON THINKING FOR ONESELF

A library may be very large; but if it is in disorder, it is not so useful as one that is small but well arranged. In the same way, a man may have a great mass of knowledge, but if he has not worked it up by thinking it over for himself, it has much less value than a far smaller amount which he has thoroughly pondered. For it is only when a man looks at his knowledge from all sides, and combines the things he knows by comparing truth with truth, that he obtains a complete hold over it and gets it into his power. A man cannot turn over anything in his mind unless he knows it; he should, therefore, learn something; but it is only when he has turned it over that he can be said to know it.

Reading and learning are things that anyone can do of his own free will; but not so *thinking*. Thinking must be kindled, like a fire by a draught; it must be sustained by some interest in the matter in hand. This interest may be of purely objective kind, or merely subjective. The latter comes into play only in things that concern us personally. Objective interest is confined to heads that think by nature; to whom thinking is as natural as breathing; and they are very rare. This is why most men of learning show so little of it.

It is incredible what a different effect is produced upon the mind by thinking for oneself, as compared with reading. It carries on and intensifies that original difference in the nature of two minds which leads the one to think and the other to read. What I mean is that reading forces alien thoughts upon the mind - thoughts which are as foreign to the drift and temper in which it may be for the moment, as the seal is to the wax on which it stamps its imprint. The mind is thus entirely under compulsion from without; it is driven to think this or that, though for the moment it may not have the slightest impulse or inclination to do so.

But when a man thinks for himself, he follows the impulse of his own mind, which is determined for him at the time, either by his environment or some particular recollection. The visible world of a man's surroundings does not, as reading does, impress a *single* definite thought upon his mind, but merely gives the matter and occasion which lead him to think what is appropriate to his nature and present temper. So it is, that much reading deprives the mind of all elasticity; it is like keeping a spring continually under pressure. The safest way of having no thoughts of one's own is to take up a book every moment one has nothing else to do. It is this practice which explains why erudition makes most men more stupid and silly than they are by nature, and prevents their writings obtaining any measure of success. They remain, in Pope's words:

For ever reading, never to be read! (*Dunciad*, iii, 194)

Men of learning are those who have done their reading in the pages of a book. Thinkers and men of genius are those who have gone straight to the book of Nature; it is they who have enlightened the world and carried humanity further on its way. If a man's thoughts are to have truth and life in them, they must, after all, be his own fundamental thoughts; for these are the only ones that he can fully and wholly understand. To read another's thoughts is like taking the leavings of a meal to which we have not been invited, or putting on the clothes which some unknown visitor has laid aside. The thought we read is related to the thought which springs up in ourselves, as the fossil-impress of some prehistoric plant to a plant as it buds forth in spring-time.

Reading is nothing more than a substitute for thought of one's own. It means putting the mind into leading-strings. The multitude of books serves only to show how many false paths there are, and how widely astray a man may wander if he follows any of them. But he who is guided by his genius, he who thinks for himself, who thinks spontaneously and exactly, possesses the only compass by which he can steer aright. A man should read only when his own thoughts stagnate at their source, which will happen often enough even with the best of minds. On the other hand, to take up a book for the purpose of scaring away one's own original thoughts is sin against the Holy Spirit. It is like running away from Nature to look at a museum of dried plants or gaze at a landscape in copperplate.

A man may have discovered some portion of truth or wisdom, after spending a great deal of time and trouble in thinking it over for himself and adding thought to thought; and it may sometimes happen that he could have found it all ready to hand in a book and spared himself the trouble. But even so, it is a hundred times more valuable if he has acquired it by thinking it out for himself. For it is only when we gain our knowledge in this way that it enters as an integral part, a living member, into the whole system of our thought; that it stands in complete and firm relation with what we know; that it is understood with all that underlies it and follows from it; that it wears the color, the precise shade, the distinguishing mark, of our own way of thinking; that it comes exactly at the right time, just as we felt the necessity for it; that it stands fast and cannot be forgotten. This is the perfect application, nay, the interpretation, of Goethe's advice to earn our inheritance for ourselves so that we may really possess it:

> *Was due ererbt von deinen Välern hast, Erwirb es, um es zu besitzen.* (*Faust*, I. 329).

The man who thinks for himself, forms his own opinions and learns the authorities for them only later on, when they serve but to strengthen his belief in them and in himself. But the book-philosopher starts from the authorities. He reads other people's books, collects their opinions, and so forms a whole for himself, which resembles an automaton made up of anything but flesh and blood. Contrarily, he who thinks for himself creates a work like a living man as made by Nature. For the work comes into being as a man does; the thinking mind is impregnated from without, and it then forms and bears its child.

Truth that has been merely learned is like an artificial limb, a false tooth, a waxen nose; at best, like a nose made out of another's flesh; it adheres to us only because it is put on. But truth acquired by thinking of our own is like a natural limb; it alone really belongs to us. This is the fundamental difference between the thinker and the mere man of learning. The intellectual attainments of a man who thinks for himself resemble a fine painting, where the light and shade are correct, the tone sustained, the color perfectly harmonized; it is true to life. On the other hand, the intellectual attainments of the mere man of learning are like a large palette, full of all sorts of colors, which at most are systematically arranged, but devoid of harmony, connection and meaning.

Reading is thinking with some one else's head instead of one's own. To think with one's own head is always to aim at developing a coherent whole - a system, even though it be not a strictly complete one; and nothing hinders this so much as too strong a current of others' thoughts, such as comes of continual reading. These thoughts, springing every one of them from different minds, belonging to different systems, and tinged with different colors, never of themselves flow together into an intellectual whole; they never form a unity of knowledge, or insight, or conviction; but, rather, fill the head with a Babylonian confusion of tongues. The mind that is over-loaded with alien thought is thus deprived of all clear insight, and is well-nigh disorganized. This is a state of things observable in many men of learning; and it makes them inferior in sound sense, correct judgment and practical tact, to many illiterate persons, who, after obtaining a little knowledge from without, by means of experience, inter-course with others, and a small amount of reading, have always subordinated it to, and embodied it with, their own thought.

The really scientific *thinker* does the same thing as these illiterate persons, but on a larger scale. Although he has need of much knowledge, and so must read a great deal, his mind is nevertheless strong enough to master it all, to assimilate and incorporate it with the system of his thoughts, and so to make it fit in with the organic unity of his insight, which, though vast, is always growing. And in the process, his own thought, like the bass in an organ, always dominates everything and is never drowned by other tones, as happens with minds which are full of mere antiquarian lore; where shreds of music, as it were, in every key, mingle confusedly, and no fundamental note is heard at all.

Those who have spent their lives in reading, and taken their wisdom from books, are like people who have obtained precise information about a country from the descriptions of many travellers. Such people can tell a great deal about it; but, after all, they have no connected, clear, and profound knowledge of its real condition. But those who have spent their lives in thinking, resemble the travellers themselves; they alone really know what they are talking about; they are acquainted with the actual state of affairs, and are quite at home in the subject.

The thinker stands in the same relation to the ordinary book-philosopher as an eye-witness does to the historian; he speaks from direct knowledge of his own. That is why all those who think for themselves come, at bottom, to much the same conclusion. The differences they present are due to their different points of view; and when these do not affect the matter, they all speak alike. They merely express the result of their own objective perception of things. There are many passages in my works which I have given to the public only after some hesitation, because of their paradoxical nature; and afterwards I have experienced a pleasant surprise in finding the same opinion recorded in the works of great men who lived long ago.

The book-philosopher merely reports what one person has said and another meant, or the objections raised by a third, and so on. He compares different opinions, ponders, criticises, and tries to get at the truth of the matter; herein on a par with the critical historian. For instance, he will set out to inquire whether Leibnitz was not for some time a follower of Spinoza, and questions of a like nature. The curious student of such matters may find conspicuous examples of what I mean in Herbart's *Analytical Elucidation of Morality and Natural Right,* and in the same author's *Letters on Freedom.* Surprise may be felt that a man of the kind should put himself to so much trouble; for, on the face of it, if he would only examine the matter for himself, he would speedily attain his object by the exercise of a little thought. But there is a small difficulty in the way. It does not depend upon his own will. A man can always sit down and read, but not – think. It is with thoughts as with men; they cannot always be summoned at pleasure; we must wait for them to come. Thought about a subject must appear of itself, by a happy and harmonious combination of external stimulus with mental temper and attention; and it is just that which never seems to come to these people.

This truth may be illustrated by what happens in the case of matters affecting our own personal interest. When it is necessary to come to some resolution in a matter of that kind, we cannot well sit down at any given moment and think over the merits of the case and make up our mind; for, if we try to do so, we often find ourselves unable, at that particular moment, to keep our mind fixed upon the subject; it wanders off to other things. Aversion to the matter in question is sometimes to blame for this. In such a case we should not use force, but wait for the proper frame of mind to come of itself. It often comes unexpectedly and returns again and again; and the variety of temper in which we approach it at different moments puts the matter always in a fresh light. It is this long process which is understood by the term *a ripe resolution.* For the work of coming to a resolution must be distributed; and in the process much that is overlooked at one moment occurs to us at another; and the repugnance vanishes when we find, as we usually do, on a closer inspection, that things are not so bad as they seemed.

This rule applies to the life of the intellect as well as to matters of practice. A man must wait for the right moment. Not even the greatest mind is capable of thinking for itself at all times. Hence a great mind does well to spend its leisure in reading, which, as I have said, is a substitute for thought; it brings stuff to the mind by letting another person do the thinking; although that is always done in a manner not our own. Therefore, a man should not read too much, in order that his mind may not become accustomed to the substitute and thereby forget the reality; that it may not form the habit of walking in well-worn paths; nor by following an alien course of thought grow a stranger to its own. Least of all should a man quite withdraw his gaze from the real world for the mere sake of reading; as the impulse and the temper which prompt to thought of one's own come far oftener from the world of reality than from the world of books. The real life that a man sees before him is the natural subject of thought; and in its strength as the primary element of existence, it can more easily than anything else rouse and influence the thinking mind.

After these considerations, it will not be matter for surprise that a man who thinks for himself can easily be distinguished from the book-philosopher by the very way in which he talks, by his marked earnestness, and the originality, directness, and personal conviction that stamp all his thoughts and expressions. The book-philosopher, on the other hand, lets it be seen that everything he has is second-hand; that his ideas are like the number and trash of an old furniture-shop, collected together from all quarters. Mentally, he is dull and pointless – a copy of a copy.

His literary style is made up of conventional, nay, vulgar phrases, and terms that happen to be current; in this respect much like a small State where all the money that circulates is foreign, because it has no coinage of its own.

Mere experience can as little as reading supply the place of thought. It stands to thinking in the same relation in which eating stands to digestion and assimilation. When experience boasts that to its discoveries alone is due the advancement of the human race, it is as though the mouth were to claim the whole credit of maintaining the body in health.

The works of all truly capable minds are distinguished by a character of *decision* and *definiteness*, which means they are clear and free from obscurity. A truly capable mind always knows definitely and clearly what it is that it wants to express, whether its medium is prose, verse, or music. Other minds are not decisive and not definite; and by this they may be known for what they are.

The characteristic sign of a mind of the highest order is that it always judges at first hand. Everything it advances is the result of thinking for itself; and this is everywhere evident by the way in which it gives its thoughts utterance. Such a mind is like a Prince. In the realm of intellect its authority is imperial, whereas the authority of minds of a lower order is delegated only; as may be seen in their style, which has no independent stamp of its own.

Every one who really thinks for himself is so far like a monarch. His position is undelegated and supreme. His judgments, like royal decrees, spring from his own sovereign power and proceed directly from himself. He acknowledges authority as little as a monarch admits a command; he subscribes to nothing but what he has himself authorized. The multitude of common minds, laboring under all sorts of current opinions, authorities, prejudices, is like the people, which silently obeys the law and accepts orders from above.

Those who are so zealous and eager to settle debated questions by citing authorities, are really glad when they are able to put the understanding and the insight of others into the field in place of their own, which are wanting. Their number is legion. For, as Seneca says, there is no man but prefers belief to the exercise of judgment – *unusquisque mavult credere quam judicare.* In their controversies such people make a promiscuous use of the weapon of authority, and strike out at one another with it. If any one chances to become involved in such a contest, he will do well not to try reason and argument as a mode of defence; for against a weapon of that kind these people are like Siegfrieds, with a skin of horn, and dipped in the flood of incapacity for thinking and judging. They will meet his attack by bringing up their authorities as a way of abashing him – *argumentum ad verecundiam,* and then cry out that they have won the battle.

In the real world, be it never so fair, favorable and pleasant, we always live subject to the law of gravity which we have to be constantly overcoming. But in the world of intellect we are disembodied spirits, held in bondage to no such law, and free from penury and distress. Thus it is that there exists no happiness on earth like that which, at the auspicious moment, a fine and fruitful mind finds in itself.

The presence of a thought is like the presence of a woman we love. We fancy we shall never forget the thought nor become indifferent to the dear one. But out of sight, out of mind! The finest thought runs the risk of being irrevocably forgotten if we do not write it down, and the darling of being deserted if we do not marry her.

There are plenty of thoughts which are valuable to the man who thinks them; but only few of them which have enough strength to produce repercussive or reflect action – I mean, to win the reader's sympathy after they have been put on paper.

But still it must not be forgotten that a true value attaches only to what a man has thought in the first instance *for his own case.* Thinkers may be classed according as they think chiefly for their own case or for that of others. The former are the genuine independent thinkers; they really think and are really independent; they are the true *philosophers;* they alone are in earnest. The pleasure and the happiness of their existence consists in thinking. The others are the *sophists;* they want to seem that which they are not, and seek their happiness in what they hope to get from the world. They are in earnest about nothing else. To which of these two classes a man belongs may be seen by his whole style and manner. Lichtenberg is an example for the former class; Herder, there can be no doubt, belongs to the second.

When one considers how vast and how close to us is *the problem of existence* – this equivocal, tortured, fleeting, dream-like existence of ours – so vast and so close that a man no sooner discovers it than it overshadows and obscures all other problems and aims; and when one sees how all men, with few and rare exceptions, have no clear consciousness of the problem, nay, seem to be quite unaware of its presence, but busy themselves with everything rather than with this, and live on, taking no thought but for the passing day and the hardly longer span of their own personal future, either expressly discarding the problem or else over-ready to come to terms with it by adopting some system of popular metaphysics and letting it satisfy them; when, I say, one takes all this to heart, one may come to the opinion that man may be said to be *a thinking being* only in a very remote sense, and henceforth feel no special surprise at any trait of human thoughtlessness or folly; but know, rather, that the normal man's intellectual range of vision does indeed extend beyond that of the brute, whose whole existence is, as it were, a continual present, with no consciousness of the past or the future, but not such an immeasurable distance as is generally supposed.

This is, in fact, corroborated by the way in which most men converse; where their thoughts are found to be chopped up fine, like chaff, so that for them to spin out a discourse of any length is impossible.

If this world were peopled by really thinking beings, it could not be that noise of every kind would be allowed such generous limits, as is the case with the most horrible and at the same time aimless form of it.[1] If Nature had meant man to think, she would not have given him ears; or, at any rate, she would have furnished them with airtight flaps, such as are the enviable possession of the bat. But, in truth, man is a poor animal like the rest, and his powers are meant only to maintain him in the struggle for existence; so he must need keep his ears always open, to announce of themselves, by night as by day, the approach of the pursuer.

In the drama, which is the most perfect reflection of human existence, there are three stages in the presentation of the subject, with a corresponding variety in the design and scope of the piece.

At the first, which is also the most common, stage, the drama is never anything more than merely *interesting*. The persons gain our attention by following their own aims, which resemble ours; the action advances by means of intrigue and the play of character and incident; while wit and raillery season the whole.

At the second stage, the drama becomes *sentimental*. Sympathy is roused with the hero and, indirectly, with ourselves. The action takes a pathetic turn; but the end is peaceful and satisfactory.

The climax is reached with the third stage, which is the most difficult. There the drama aims at being *tragic*. We are brought face to face with great suffering and the storm and stress of existence; and the outcome of it is to show the vanity of all human effort. Deeply moved, we are either directly prompted to disengage our will from the struggle of life, or else a chord is struck in us which echoes a similar feeling.

The beginning, it is said, is always difficult. In the drama it is just the contrary; for these the difficulty always lies in the end. This is proved by countless plays which promise very well for the first act or two, and then become muddled, stick or falter - notoriously so in the fourth act - and finally conclude in a way that is either forced or unsatisfactory or else long foreseen by every one. Sometimes, too, the end is positively revolting, as in

Lessing's *Emilia Galotti*, which sends the spectators home in a temper.

This difficulty in regard to the end of a play arises partly because it is everywhere easier to get things into a tangle than to get them out again; partly also because at the beginning we give the author *carte blanche* to do as he likes, but, at the end, make certain definite demands upon him. Thus we ask for a conclusion that shall be either quite happy or else quite tragic; whereas human affairs do not easily take so decided a turn; and then we expect that it shall be natural, fit and proper, unlabored, and at the same time foreseen by no one.

These remarks are also applicable to an epic and to a novel; but the more compact nature of the drama makes the difficulty plainer by increasing it.

E nihilo nihil fit. That nothing can come from nothing is a maxim true in fine art as elsewhere. In composing an historical picture, a good artist will use living men as a model, and take the groundwork of the faces from life; and then proceed to idealize them in point of beauty or expression. A similar method, I fancy, is adopted by good novelists. In drawing a character they take a general outline of it from some real person of their acquaintance, and then idealize and complete it to suit their purpose.

A novel will be of a high and noble order, the more it represents of inner, and the less it represents of outer, life; and the ratio between the two will supply a means of judging any novel, of whatever kind, from *Tristram Shandy* down to the crudest and most sensational tale of knight or robber. *Tristram Shandy* has, indeed, as good as no action at all; and there is not much in *La Nouvelle Heloïse* and *Wilhelm Meister*. Even *Don Quixote* has relatively little; and what there is, very unimportant, and introduced merely for the sake of fun. And these four are the best of all existing novels.

Consider, further, the wonderful romances of Jean Paul, and how much inner life is shown on the narrowest basis of actual event. Even in Walter Scott's novels there is a great preponderance of inner over outer life, and incident is never brought in except for the purpose of giving play to thought and emotion; whereas, in bad novels, incident is there on its own account. Skill consists in setting the inner life in motion with the smallest possible array of circumstance; for it is this inner life that really excites our interest.

The business of the novelist is not to relate great events, but to make small ones interesting.

History, which I like to think of as the contrary of poetry [Greek: istoroumenon - pepoiaemenon], is for time what geography is for space; and it is no more to be called a science, in any strict sense of the word, than is geography, because it does not deal with universal truths, but only with particular details. History has always been the favorite study of those who wish to learn something, without having to face the effort demanded by any branch of real knowledge, which taxes the intelligence. In our time history is a favorite pursuit; as witness the numerous books upon the subject which appear every year.

If the reader cannot help thinking, with me, that history is merely the constant recurrence of similar things, just as in a kaleidoscope the same bits of glass are represented, but in different combinations, he will not be able to share all this lively interest; nor, however, will he censure it. But there is a ridiculous and absurd claim, made by many people, to regard history as a part of philosophy, nay, as philosophy itself; they imagine that history can take its place.

The preference shown for history by the greater public in all ages may be illustrated by the kind of conversation which is so much in vogue everywhere in society. It generally consists in one person relating something and then another person relating something else; so that in this way everyone is sure of receiving attention. Both here and in the case of history it is plain that the mind is occupied with particular details. But as in science, so also in every worthy conversation, the mind rises to the consideration of some general truth.

This objection does not, however, deprive history of its value. Human life is short and fleeting, and many millions of individuals share in it, who are swallowed by that monster of oblivion which is waiting for them with ever-open jaws. It is thus a very thankworthy task to try to rescue something - the memory of interesting and important events, or the leading features and personages of some epoch - from the general shipwreck of the world.

From another point of view, we might look upon history as the sequel to zoology; for while with all other animals it is enough to observe the species, with man individuals, and therefore individual events have to be studied; because every man possesses a character as an individual. And since individuals and events are without number or end, an essential imperfection attaches to history. In the study of it, all that a man learns never contributes to lessen that which he has still to learn. With any real science, a perfection of knowledge is, at any rate, conceivable.

When we gain access to the histories of China and of India, the endlessness of the subject-matter will reveal to us the defects in the study, and force our historians to see that the object of science is to recognize the many in the one, to perceive the rules in any given example, and to apply to the life of nations a knowledge of mankind; not to go on counting up facts *ad infinitum*.

There are two kinds of history; the history of politics and the history of literature and art. The one is the history of the will; the other, that of the intellect. The first is a tale of woe, even of terror: it is a record of agony, struggle, fraud, and horrible murder *en masse*. The second is everywhere pleasing and serene, like the intellect when left to itself, even though its path be one of error. Its chief branch is the history of philosophy. This is, in fact, its fundamental bass, and the notes of it are heard even in the other kind of history. These deep tones guide the formation of opinion, and opinion rules the world. Hence philosophy, rightly understood, is a material force of the most powerful kind, though very slow in its working. The philosophy of a period is thus the fundamental bass of its history.

The NEWSPAPER, is the second-hand in the clock of history; and it is not only made of baser metal than those which point to the minute and the hour, but it seldom goes right.

The so-called leading article is the chorus to the drama of passing events.

Exaggeration of every kind is as essential to journalism as it is to the dramatic art; for the object of journalism is to make events go as far as possible. Thus it is that all journalists are, in the very nature of their calling, alarmists; and this is their way of giving interest to what they write. Herein they are like little dogs; if anything stirs, they immediately set up a shrill bark.

Therefore, let us carefully regulate the attention to be paid to this trumpet of danger, so that it may not disturb our digestion. Let us recognize that a newspaper is at best but a magnifying-glass, and very often merely a shadow on the wall.

The *pen* is to thought what the stick is to walking; but you walk most easily when you have no stick, and you think with the greatest perfection when you have no pen in your hand. It is only when a man begins to be old that he likes to use a stick and is glad to take up his pen.

When an *hypothesis* has once come to birth in the mind, or gained a footing there, it leads a life so far comparable with the life of an organism, as that it assimilates matter from the outer world only when it is like in kind with it and beneficial; and when, contrarily, such matter is not like in kind but hurtful, the hypothesis, equally with the organism, throws it off, or, if forced to take it, gets rid of it again entire.

To gain *immortality* an author must possess so many excellences that while it will not be easy to find anyone to understand and appreciate them all, there will be men in every age who are able to recognize and value some of them. In this way the credit of his book will be maintained throughout the long course of centuries, in spite of the fact that human interests are always changing.

An author like this, who has a claim to the continuance of his life even with posterity, can only be a man who, over the wide earth, will seek his like in vain, and offer a palpable contrast with everyone else in virtue of his unmistakable distinction. Nay, more: were he, like the wandering Jew, to live through several generations, he would still remain in the same superior position. If this were not so, it would be difficult to see why his thoughts should not perish like those of other men.

Metaphors and *similes* are of great value, in so far as they explain an unknown relation by a known one. Even the more detailed simile which grows into a parable or an allegory, is nothing more than the exhibition of some relation in its simplest, most visible and palpable form. The growth of ideas rests, at bottom, upon similes; because ideas arise by a process of combining the similarities and neglecting the differences between things. Further, intelligence, in the strict sense of the word, ultimately consists in a seizing of relations; and a clear and pure grasp of relations is all the more often attained when the comparison is made between cases that lie wide apart from one another, and between things of quite different nature. As long as a relation is known to me as existing only in a single case, I have but an *individual* idea of it - in other words, only an intuitive knowledge of it; but as soon as I see the same relation in two different cases, I have a *general* idea of its whole nature, and this is a deeper and more perfect knowledge.

Since, then, similes and metaphors are such a powerful engine of knowledge, it is a sign of great intelligence in a writer if his similes are unusual and, at the same time, to the point. Aristotle also observes that by far the most important thing to a writer is to have this power of metaphor; for it is a gift which cannot be acquired, and it is a mark of genius.

As regards *reading*, to require that a man shall retain everything he has ever read, is like asking him to carry about with him all he has ever eaten. The one kind of food has given him bodily, and the other mental, nourishment; and it is through these two means that he has grown to be what he is. The body assimilates only that which is like it; and so a man retains in his mind only that which interests him, in other words, that which suits his system of thought or his purposes in life.

If a man wants to read good books, he must make a point of avoiding bad ones; for life is short, and time and energy limited.

Repetitio est mater studiorum. Any book that is at all important ought to be at once read through twice; partly because, on a second reading, the connection of the different portions of the book will be better understood, and the beginning comprehended only when the end is known; and partly because we are not in the same temper and disposition on both readings. On the second perusal we get a new view of every passage and a different impression of the whole book, which then appears in another light.

A man's works are the quintessence of his mind, and even though he may possess very great capacity, they will always be incomparably more valuable than his conversation. Nay, in all essential matters his works will not only make up for the lack of personal intercourse with him, but they will far surpass it in solid advantages. The writings even of a man of moderate genius may be edifying, worth reading and instructive, because they are his quintessence - the result and fruit of all his thought and study; whilst conversation with him may be unsatisfactory.

So it is that we can read books by men in whose company we find nothing to please, and that a high degree of culture leads us to seek entertainment almost wholly from books and not from men.

NOTES

1. *Translator's Note.* - Schopenhauer refers to the cracking of whips. See the Essay *On Noise* in *Studies in Pessimism*.

ON CRITICISM

The following brief remarks on the critical faculty are chiefly intended to show that, for the most part, there is no such thing. It is a *rara avis;* almost as rare, indeed, as the phoenix, which appears only once in five hundred years.

When we speak of *taste* - an expression not chosen with any regard for it - we mean the discovery, or, it may be only the recognition, of what is *right aesthetically*, apart from the guidance of any rule; and this, either because no rule has as yet been extended to the matter in question, or else because, if existing, it is unknown to the artist, or the critic, as the case may be. Instead of *taste,* we might use the expression *aesthetic sense*, if this were not tautological.

The perceptive critical taste is, so to speak, the female analogue to the male quality of productive talent or genius. Not capable of *begetting* great work itself, it consists in a capacity of *reception*, that is to say, of recognizing as such what is right, fit, beautiful, or the reverse; in other words, of discriminating the good from the bad, of discovering and appreciating the one and condemning the other.

In appreciating a genius, criticism should not deal with the errors in his productions or with the poorer of his works, and then proceed to rate him low; it should attend only to the qualities in which he most excels. For in the sphere of intellect, as in other spheres, weakness and perversity cleave so firmly to human nature that even the most brilliant mind is not wholly and at all times free from them. Hence the great errors to be found even in the works of the greatest men; or as Horace puts it, *quandoque bonus dormitat Homerus.*

That which distinguishes genius, and should be the standard for judging it, is the height to which it is able to soar when it is in the proper mood and finds a fitting occasion - a height always out of the reach of ordinary talent. And, in like manner, it is a very dangerous thing to compare two great men of the same class; for instance, two great poets, or musicians, or philosophers, or artists; because injustice to the one or the other, at least for the moment, can hardly be avoided. For in making a comparison of the kind the critic looks to some particular merit of the one and at once discovers that it is absent in the other, who is thereby disparaged. And then if the process is reversed, and the critic begins with the latter and discovers his peculiar merit, which is quite of a different order from that presented by the former, with whom it may be looked for in vain, the result is that both of them suffer undue depreciation.

There are critics who severally think that it rests with each one of them what shall be accounted good, and what bad. They all mistake their own toy-trumpets for the trombones of fame.

A drug does not effect its purpose if the dose is too large; and it is the same with censure and adverse criticism when it exceeds the measure of justice.

The disastrous thing for intellectual merit is that it must wait for those to praise the good who have themselves produced nothing but what is bad; nay, it is a primary misfortune that it has to receive its crown at the hands of the critical power of mankind - a quality of which most men possess only the weak and impotent semblance, so that the reality may be numbered amongst the rarest gifts of nature. Hence La Bruyère's remark is, unhappily, as true as it is neat. *Après l'esprit de discernement,* he says, *ce qu'il y a au monde de plus rare, ce sont les diamans et les perles*. The spirit of discernment! the critical faculty! it is these that are lacking. Men do not know how to distinguish the genuine from the false, the corn from the chaff, gold from copper; or to perceive the wide gulf that separates a genius from an ordinary man. Thus we have that bad state of things described in an old-fashioned verse, which gives it as the lot of the great ones here on earth to be recognized only when they are gone:

> *Es ist nun das Geschick der Grossen fiier auf Erden, Erst wann sie nicht mehr sind; von uns erkannt zu werden.*

When any genuine and excellent work makes its appearance, the chief difficulty in its way is the amount of bad work it finds already in possession of the field, and accepted as though it were good. And then if, after a long time, the new comer really succeeds, by a hard struggle, in vindicating his place for himself and winning reputation, he will soon encounter fresh difficulty from some affected, dull, awkward imitator, whom people drag in, with the object of calmly setting him up on the altar beside the genius; not seeing the difference and really thinking that here they have to do with another great man. This is what Yriarte means by the first lines of his twenty-eighth Fable, where he declares that the ignorant rabble always sets equal value on the good and the bad:

> *Siempre acostumbra hacer el vulgo necio De lo bueno y lo malo igual aprecio.*

So even Shakespeare's dramas had, immediately after his death, to give place to those of Ben Jonson, Massinger, Beaumont and Fletcher, and to yield the supremacy for a hundred years. So Kant's serious philosophy was crowded out by the nonsense of Fichte, Schelling, Jacobi, Hegel. And even in a sphere accessible to all, we have seen unworthy imitators quickly diverting public attention from the incomparable Walter Scott. For, say what you will, the public has no sense for excellence, and therefore no notion how very rare it is to find men really capable of doing anything great in poetry, philosophy, or art, or that their works are alone worthy of exclusive attention. The dabblers, whether in verse or in any other high sphere, should be every day unsparingly reminded that neither gods, nor men, nor booksellers have pardoned their mediocrity:

> *mediocribus esse poetis Non homines, non Dî, non concessere columnae.*[1]

Are they not the weeds that prevent the corn coming up, so that they may cover all the ground themselves? And then there happens that which has been well and freshly described by the lamented Feuchtersleben,[2] who died so young: how people cry out in their haste that nothing is being done, while all the while great work is quietly growing to maturity; and then, when it appears, it is not seen or heard in the clamor, but goes its way silently, in modest grief:

> *"Ist doch" – rufen sie vermessen –*
> *Nichts im Werke, nichts gethan!"*
> *Und das Grosse, reift indessen*
> *Still heran.*
> *Es ersheint nun: niemand sieht es,*
> *Niemand hört es im Geschrei*
> *Mit bescheid'ner Trauer zieht es*
> *Still vorbei.*

This lamentable death of the critical faculty is not less obvious in the case of science, as is shown by the tenacious life of false and disproved theories. If they are once accepted, they may go on bidding defiance to truth for fifty or even a hundred years and more, as stable as an iron pier in the midst of the waves. The Ptolemaic system was still held a century after Copernicus had promulgated his theory. Bacon, Descartes and Locke made their way extremely slowly and only after a long time; as the reader may see by d'Alembert's celebrated Preface to the *Encyclopedia.*

Newton was not more successful; and this is sufficiently proved by the bitterness and contempt with which Leibnitz attacked his theory of gravitation in the controversy with Clarke.[3] Although Newton lived for almost forty years after the appearance of the *Principia*, his teaching was, when he died, only to some extent accepted in his own country, whilst outside England he counted scarcely twenty adherents; if we may believe the introductory note to Voltaire's exposition of his theory. It was, indeed, chiefly owing to this treatise of Voltaire's that the system became known in France nearly twenty years after Newton's death. Until then a firm, resolute, and patriotic stand was made by the Cartesian *Vortices*; whilst only forty years previously, this same Cartesian philosophy had been forbidden in the French schools; and now in turn d'Agnesseau, the Chancellor, refused Voltaire the *Imprimatur* for his treatise on the Newtonian doctrine. On the other hand, in our day Newton's absurd theory of color still completely holds the field, forty years after the publication of Goethe's. Hume, too, was disregarded up to his fiftieth year, though he began very early and wrote in a thoroughly popular style. And Kant, in spite of having written and talked all his life long, did not become a famous man until he was sixty.

Artists and poets have, to be sure, more chance than thinkers, because their public is at least a hundred times as large. Still, what was thought of Beethoven and Mozart during their lives? what of Dante? what even of Shakespeare? If the latter's contemporaries had in any way recognized his worth, at least one good and accredited portrait of him would have come down to us from an age when the art of painting flourished; whereas we possess only some very doubtful pictures, a bad copperplate, and a still worse bust on his tomb.[4] And in like manner, if he had been duly honored, specimens of his handwriting would have been preserved to us by the hundred, instead of being confined, as is the case, to the signatures to a few legal documents. The Portuguese are still proud of their only poet Camoëns. He lived, however, on alms collected every evening in the street by a black slave whom he had brought with him from the Indies. In time, no doubt, justice will be done everyone; *tempo è galant uomo*; but it is as late and slow in arriving as in a court of law, and the secret condition of it is that the recipient shall be no longer alive. The precept of Jesus the son of Sirach is faithfully followed: *Judge none blessed before his death.*[5] He, then, who has produced immortal works, must find comfort by applying to them the words of the Indian myth, that the minutes of life amongst the immortals seem like years of earthly existence; and so, too, that years upon earth are only as the minutes of the immortals.

This lack of critical insight is also shown by the fact that, while in every century the excellent work of earlier time is held in honor, that of its own is misunderstood, and the attention which is its due is given to bad work, such as every decade carries with it only to be the sport of the next. That men are slow to recognize genuine merit when it appears in their own age, also proves that they do not understand or enjoy or really value the long-acknowledged works of genius, which they honor only on the score of authority. The crucial test is the fact that bad work – Fichte's philosophy, for example – if it wins any reputation, also maintains it for one or two generations; and only when its public is very large does its fall follow sooner.

Now, just as the sun cannot shed its light but to the eye that sees it, nor music sound but to the hearing ear, so the value of all masterly work in art and science is conditioned by the kinship and capacity of the mind to which it speaks. It is only such a mind as this that possesses the magic word to stir and call forth the spirits that lie hidden in great work. To the ordinary mind a masterpiece is a sealed cabinet of mystery, – an unfamiliar musical instrument from which the player, however much he may flatter himself, can draw none but confused tones. How different a painting looks when seen in a good light, as compared with some dark corner! Just in the same way, the impression made by a masterpiece varies with the capacity of the mind to understand it.

A fine work, then, requires a mind sensitive to its beauty; a thoughtful work, a mind that can really think, if it is to exist and live at all. But alas! it may happen only too often that he who gives a fine work to the world afterwards feels like a maker of fireworks, who displays with enthusiasm the wonders that have taken him so much time and trouble to prepare, and then learns that he has come to the wrong place, and that the fancied spectators were one and all inmates of an asylum for the blind. Still even that is better than if his public had consisted entirely of men who made fireworks themselves; as in this case, if his display had been extraordinarily good, it might possibly have cost him his head.

The source of all pleasure and delight is the feeling of kinship. Even with the sense of beauty it is unquestionably our own species in the animal world, and then again our own race, that appears to us the fairest. So, too, in intercourse with others, every man shows a decided preference for those who resemble him; and a blockhead will find the society of another blockhead incomparably more pleasant than that of any number of great minds put together. Every man must necessarily take his chief pleasure in his own work, because it is the mirror of his own mind, the echo of his own thought; and next in order will come the work of people like him; that is to say, a dull, shallow and perverse man, a dealer in mere words, will give his sincere and hearty applause only to that which is dull, shallow, perverse or merely verbose. On the other hand, he will allow merit to the work of great minds only on the score of authority, in other words, because he is ashamed to speak his opinion; for in reality they give him no pleasure at all. They do not appeal to him; nay, they repel him; and he will not confess this even to himself. The works of genius cannot be fully enjoyed except by those who are themselves of the privileged order. The first recognition of them, however, when they exist without authority to support them, demands considerable superiority of mind.

When the reader takes all this into consideration, he should be surprised, not that great work is so late in winning reputation, but that it wins it at all. And as a matter of fact, fame comes only by a slow and complex process. The stupid person is by degrees forced, and as it were, tamed, into recognizing the superiority of one who stands immediately above him; this one in his turn bows before some one else; and so it goes on until the weight of the votes gradually prevail over their number; and this is just the condition of all genuine, in other words, deserved fame. But until then, the greatest genius, even after he has passed his time of trial, stands like a king amidst a crowd of his own subjects, who do not know him by sight and therefore will not do his behests; unless, indeed, his chief ministers of state are in his train. For no subordinate official can be the direct recipient of the royal commands, as he knows only the signature of his immediate superior; and this is repeated all the way up into the highest ranks, where the under-secretary attests the minister's signature, and the minister that of the king. There are analogous stages to be passed before a genius can attain widespread fame. This is why his reputation most easily comes to a standstill at the very outset; because the highest authorities, of whom there can be but few, are most frequently not to be found; but the further down he goes in the scale the more numerous are those who take the word from above, so that his fame is no more arrested.

We must console ourselves for this state of things by reflecting that it is really fortunate that the greater number of men do not form a judgment on their own responsibility, but merely take it on authority. For what sort of criticism should we have on Plato and Kant, Homer, Shakespeare and Goethe, if every man were to form his opinion by what he really has and enjoys of these writers, instead of being forced by authority to speak of them in a fit and proper way, however little he may really feel what he says. Unless something of this kind took place, it would be impossible for true merit, in any high sphere, to attain fame at all. At the same time it is also fortunate that every man has just so much critical power of his own as is necessary for recognizing the superiority of those who are placed immediately over him, and for following their lead. This means that the many come in the end to submit to the authority of the few; and there results that hierarchy of critical judgments on which is based the possibility of a steady, and eventually wide-reaching, fame.

The lowest class in the community is quite impervious to the merits of a great genius; and for these people there is nothing left but the monument raised to him, which, by the impression it produces on their senses, awakes in them a dim idea of the man's greatness.

Literary journals should be a dam against the unconscionable scribbling of the age, and the ever-increasing deluge of bad and useless books. Their judgments should be uncorrupted, just and rigorous; and every piece of bad work done by an incapable person; every device by which the empty head tries to come to the assistance of the empty purse, that is to say, about nine-tenths of all existing books, should be mercilessly scourged. Literary journals would then perform their duty, which is to keep down the craving for writing and put a check upon the deception of the public, instead of furthering these evils by a miserable toleration, which plays into the hands of author and publisher, and robs the reader of his time and his money.

If there were such a paper as I mean, every bad writer, every brainless compiler, every plagiarist from other's books, every hollow and incapable place-hunter, every sham-philosopher, every vain and languishing poetaster, would shudder at the prospect of the pillory in which his bad work would inevitably have to stand soon after publication. This would paralyze his twitching fingers, to the true welfare of literature, in which what is bad is not only useless but positively pernicious. Now, most books are bad and ought to have remained unwritten. Consequently praise should be as rare as is now the case with blame, which is withheld under the influence of personal considerations, coupled with the maxim *accedas socius, laudes lauderis ut absens*.

It is quite wrong to try to introduce into literature the same toleration as must necessarily prevail in society towards those stupid, brainless people who everywhere swarm in it. In literature such people are impudent intruders; and to disparage the bad is here duty towards the good; for he who thinks nothing bad will think nothing good either. Politeness, which has its source in social relations, is in literature an alien, and often injurious, element; because it exacts that bad work shall be called good. In this way the very aim of science and art is directly frustrated.

The ideal journal could, to be sure, be written only by people who joined incorruptible honesty with rare knowledge and still rarer power of judgment; so that perhaps there could, at the very most, be one, and even hardly one, in the whole country; but there it would stand, like a just Aeropagus, every member of which would have to be elected by all the others. Under the system that prevails at present, literary journals are carried on by a clique, and secretly perhaps also by booksellers for the good of the trade; and they are often nothing but coalitions of bad heads to prevent the good ones succeeding. As Goethe once remarked to me, nowhere is there so much dishonesty as in literature.

But, above all, anonymity, that shield of all literary rascality, would have to disappear. It was introduced under the pretext of protecting the honest critic, who warned the public, against the resentment of the author and his friends. But where there is one case of this sort, there will be a hundred where it merely serves to take all responsibility from the man who cannot stand by what he has said, or possibly to conceal the shame of one who has been cowardly and base enough to recommend a book to the public for the purpose of putting money into his own pocket. Often enough it is only a cloak for covering the obscurity, incompetence and insignificance of the critic. It is incredible what impudence these fellows will show, and what literary trickery they will venture to commit, as soon as they know they are safe under the shadow of anonymity. Let me recommend a general *Anti-criticism,* a universal medicine or panacea, to put a stop to all anonymous reviewing, whether it praises the bad or blames the good: *Rascal! your name*! For a man to wrap himself up and draw his hat over his face, and then fall upon people who are walking about without any disguise - this is not the part of a gentleman, it is the part of a scoundrel and a knave.

An anonymous review has no more authority than an anonymous letter; and one should be received with the same mistrust as the other. Or shall we take the name of the man who consents to preside over what is, in the strict sense of the word, *une société anonyme* as a guarantee for the veracity of his colleagues?

Even Rousseau, in the preface to the *Nouvelle Heloïse*, declares *tout honnête homme doit avouer les livres qu'il public*; which in plain language means that every honorable man ought to sign his articles, and that no one is honorable who does not do so. How much truer this is of polemical writing, which is the general character of reviews! Riemer was quite right in the opinion he gives in his *Reminiscences of Goethe:* [6] *An overt enemy*, he says, *an enemy who meets you face to face, is an honorable man, who will treat you fairly, and with whom you can come to terms and be reconciled: but an enemy who conceals himself* is a base, cowardly scoundrel, *who has not courage enough to avow his own judgment; it is not his opinion that he cares about, but only the secret pleasures of wreaking his anger without being found out or punished.* This will also have been Goethe's opinion, as he was generally the source from which Riemer drew his observations. And, indeed, Rousseau's maxim applies to every line that is printed. Would a man in a mask ever be allowed to harangue a mob, or speak in any assembly; and that, too, when he was going to attack others and overwhelm them with abuse?

Anonymity is the refuge for all literary and journalistic rascality. It is a practice which must be completely stopped. Every article, even in a newspaper, should be accompanied by the name of its author; and the editor should be made strictly responsible for the accuracy of the signature. The freedom of the press should be thus far restricted; so that when a man publicly proclaims through the far-sounding trumpet of the newspaper, he should be answerable for it, at any rate with his honor, if he has any; and if he has none, let his name neutralize the effect of his words. And since even the most insignificant person is known in his own circle, the result of such a measure would be to put an end to two-thirds of the newspaper lies, and to restrain the audacity of many a poisonous tongue.

NOTES

1. Horace, *Ars Poetica*, 372.
2. *Translator's Note*. - Ernst Freiherr von Feuchtersleben (1806-49), an Austrian physician, philosopher, and poet, and a specialist in medical psychology. The best known of his songs is that beginning "*Es ist bestimmt in Gottes Rath*" to which Mendelssohn composed one of his finest melodies.
3. See especially §§ 35, 113, 118, 120, 122, 128.
4. A. Wivell: *An Inquiry into the History, Authenticity, and Characteristics of Shakespeare's Portraits*; with 21 engravings. London, 1836.
5. *Ecclesiasticus*, xi. 28.
6. Preface, p. xxix.

ON REPUTATION

Writers may be classified as meteors, planets and fixed stars. A meteor makes a striking effect for a moment. You look up and cry *There!* and it is gone for ever. Planets and wandering stars last a much longer time. They often outshine the fixed stars and are confounded with them by the inexperienced; but this only because they are near. It is not long before they must yield their place; nay, the light they give is reflected only, and the sphere of their influence is confined to their own orbit – their contemporaries. Their path is one of change and movement, and with the circuit of a few years their tale is told. Fixed stars are the only ones that are constant; their position in the firmament is secure; they shine with a light of their own; their effect to-day is the same as it was yesterday, because, having no parallax, their appearance does not alter with a difference in our standpoint. They belong not to *one* system, *one* nation only, but to the universe. And just because they are so very far away, it is usually many years before their light is visible to the inhabitants of this earth.

We have seen in the previous chapter that where a man's merits are of a high order, it is difficult for him to win reputation, because the public is uncritical and lacks discernment. But another and no less serious hindrance to fame comes from the envy it has to encounter. For even in the lowest kinds of work, envy balks even the beginnings of a reputation, and never ceases to cleave to it up to the last. How great a part is played by envy in the wicked ways of the world! Ariosto is right in saying that the dark side of our mortal life predominates, so full it is of this evil:

questa assai più oscura che serena Vita mortal, tutta d'invidia piena.

For envy is the moving spirit of that secret and informal, though flourishing, alliance everywhere made by mediocrity against individual eminence, no matter of what kind. In his own sphere of work no one will allow another to be distinguished: he is an intruder who cannot be tolerated. *Si quelq'un excelle parmi nous, qu'il aille exceller ailleurs*! this is the universal password of the second-rate. In addition, then, to the rarity of true merit and the difficulty it has in being understood and recognized, there is the envy of thousands to be reckoned with, all of them bent on suppressing, nay, on smothering it altogether. No one is taken for what he is, but for what others make of him; and this is the handle used by mediocrity to keep down distinction, by not letting it come up as long as that can possibly be prevented.

There are two ways of behaving in regard to merit: either to have some of one's own, or to refuse any to others. The latter method is more convenient, and so it is generally adopted. As envy is a mere sign of deficiency, so to envy merit argues the lack of it. My excellent Balthazar Gracian has given a very fine account of this relation between envy and merit in a lengthy fable, which may be found in his *Discreto* under the heading *Hombre de ostentacion.* He describes all the birds as meeting together and conspiring against the peacock, because of his magnificent feathers. *If,* said the magpie, *we could only manage to put a stop to the cursed parading of his tail, there would soon be an end of his beauty; for what is not seen is as good as what does not exist.*

This explains how modesty came to be a virtue. It was invented only as a protection against envy. That there have always been rascals to urge this virtue, and to rejoice heartily over the bashfulness of a man of merit, has been shown at length in my chief work.[1] In Lichtenberg's *Miscellaneous Writings* I find this sentence quoted: *Modesty should be the virtue of those who possess no other.* Goethe has a well-known saying, which offends many people: *It is only knaves who are modest*! - *Nur die Lumpen sind bescheiden*! but it has its prototype in Cervantes, who includes in his *Journey up Parnassus* certain rules of conduct for poets, and amongst them the following: *Everyone whose verse shows him to be a poet should have a high opinion of himself, relying on the proverb that he is a knave who thinks himself one.* And Shakespeare, in many of his Sonnets, which gave him the only opportunity he had of speaking of himself, declares, with a confidence equal to his ingenuousness, that what he writes is immortal.[2]

A method of underrating good work often used by envy - in reality, however, only the obverse side of it - consists in the dishonorable and unscrupulous laudation of the bad; for no sooner does bad work gain currency than it draws attention from the good. But however effective this method may be for a while, especially if it is applied on a large scale, the day of reckoning comes at last, and the fleeting credit given to bad work is paid off by the lasting discredit which overtakes those who abjectly praised it. Hence these critics prefer to remain anonymous.

A like fate threatens, though more remotely, those who depreciate and censure good work; and consequently many are too prudent to attempt it. But there is another way; and when a man of eminent merit appears, the first effect he produces is often only to pique all his rivals, just as the peacock's tail offended the birds. This reduces them to a deep silence; and their silence is so unanimous that it savors of preconcertion. Their tongues are all paralyzed. It is the *silentium livoris* described by Seneca. This malicious silence, which is technically known as *ignoring*, may for a long time interfere with the growth of reputation; if, as happens in the higher walks of learning, where a man's immediate audience is wholly composed of rival workers and professed students, who then form the channel of his fame, the greater public is obliged to use its suffrage without being able to examine the matter for itself. And if, in the end, that malicious silence is broken in upon by the voice of praise, it will be but seldom that this happens entirely apart from some ulterior aim, pursued by those who thus manipulate justice. For, as Goethe says in the *West-östlicher Divan*, a man can get no recognition, either from many persons or from only one, unless it is to publish abroad the critic's own discernment:

Denn es ist kein Anerkenen,
Weder Vieler, noch des Einen,
Wenn es nicht am Tage fördert,
Wo man selbst was möchte scheinen.

The credit you allow to another man engaged in work similar to your own or akin to it, must at bottom be withdrawn from yourself; and you can praise him only at the expense of your own claims.

Accordingly, mankind is in itself not at all inclined to award praise and reputation; it is more disposed to blame and find fault, whereby it indirectly praises itself. If, notwithstanding this, praise is won from mankind, some extraneous motive must prevail. I am not here referring to the disgraceful way in which mutual friends will puff one another into a reputation; outside of that, an effectual motive is supplied by the feeling that next to the merit of doing something oneself, comes that of correctly appreciating and recognizing what others have done. This accords with the threefold division of heads drawn up by Hesiod [3] and afterwards by Machiavelli[. 4] *There are,* says the latter, *in the capacities of mankind, three varieties: one man will understand a thing by himself; another so far as it is explained to him; a third, neither of himself nor when it is put clearly before him.* He, then, who abandons hope of making good his claims to the first class, will be glad to seize the opportunity of taking a place in the second. It is almost wholly owing to this state of things that merit may always rest assured of ultimately meeting with recognition.

To this also is due the fact that when the value of a work has once been recognized and may no longer be concealed or denied, all men vie in praising and honoring it; simply because they are conscious of thereby doing themselves an honor. They act in the spirit of Xenophon's remark: *he must be a wise man who knows what is wise.* So when they see that the prize of original merit is for ever out of their reach, they hasten to possess themselves of that which comes second best - the correct appreciation of it. Here it happens as with an army which has been forced to yield; when, just as previously every man wanted to be foremost in the fight, so now every man tries to be foremost in running away. They all hurry forward to offer their applause to one who is now recognized to be worthy of praise, in virtue of a recognition, as a rule unconscious, of that law of homogeneity which I mentioned in the last chapter; so that it may seem as though their way of thinking and looking at things were homogeneous with that of the celebrated man, and that they may at least save the honor of their literary taste, since nothing else is left them.

From this it is plain that, whereas it is very difficult to win fame, it is not hard to keep it when once attained; and also that a reputation which comes quickly does not last very long; for here too, *quod cito fit, cito perit.* It is obvious that if the ordinary average man can easily recognize, and the rival workers willingly acknowledge, the value of any performance, it will not stand very much above the capacity of either of them to achieve it for themselves. *Tantum quisque laudat, quantum se posse sperat imitari* – a man will praise a thing only so far as he hopes to be able to imitate it himself. Further, it is a suspicious sign if a reputation comes quickly; for an application of the laws of homogeneity will show that such a reputation is nothing but the direct applause of the multitude. What this means may be seen by a remark once made by Phocion, when he was interrupted in a speech by the loud cheers of the mob. Turning to his friends who were standing close by, he asked: *Have I made a mistake and said something stupid?* [5]

Contrarily, a reputation that is to last a long time must be slow in maturing, and the centuries of its duration have generally to be bought at the cost of contemporary praise. For that which is to keep its position so long, must be of a perfection difficult to attain; and even to recognize this perfection requires men who are not always to be found, and never in numbers sufficiently great to make themselves heard; whereas envy is always on the watch and doing its best to smother their voice. But with moderate talent, which soon meets with recognition, there is the danger that those who possess it will outlive both it and themselves; so that a youth of fame may be followed by an old age of obscurity. In the case of great merit, on the other hand, a man may remain unknown for many years, but make up for it later on by attaining a brilliant reputation. And if it should be that this comes only after he is no more, well! he is to be reckoned amongst those of whom Jean Paul says that extreme unction is their baptism. He may console himself by thinking of the Saints, who also are canonized only after they are dead.

Thus what Mahlmann [6] has said so well in *Herodes* holds good; in this world truly great work never pleases at once, and the god set up by the multitude keeps his place on the altar but a short time:

Ich denke, das wahre Grosse in der Welt
Ist immer nur Das was nicht gleich gefällt
Und wen der Pöbel zum Gotte weiht,
Der steht auf dem Altar nur kurze Zeit.

It is worth mention that this rule is most directly confirmed in the case of pictures, where, as connoisseurs well know, the greatest masterpieces are not the first to attract attention. If they make a deep impression, it is not after one, but only after repeated, inspection; but then they excite more and more admiration every time they are seen.

Moreover, the chances that any given work will be quickly and rightly appreciated, depend upon two conditions: firstly, the character of the work, whether high or low, in other words, easy or difficult to understand; and, secondly, the kind of public it attracts, whether large or small. This latter condition is, no doubt, in most instances a, corollary of the former; but it also partly depends upon whether the work in question admits, like books and musical compositions, of being produced in great numbers. By the compound action of these two conditions, achievements which serve no materially useful end - and these alone are under consideration here - will vary in regard to the chances they have of meeting with timely recognition and due appreciation; and the order of precedence, beginning with those who have the greatest chance, will be somewhat as follows: acrobats, circus riders, ballet-dancers, jugglers, actors, singers, musicians, composers, poets (both the last on account of the multiplication of their works), architects, painters, sculptors, philosophers.

The last place of all is unquestionably taken by philosophers because their works are meant not for entertainment, but for instruction, and because they presume some knowledge on the part of the reader, and require him to make an effort of his own to understand them. This makes their public extremely small, and causes their fame to be more remarkable for its length than for its breadth. And, in general, it may be said that the possibility of a man's fame lasting a long time, stands in almost inverse ratio with the chance that it will be early in making its appearance; so that, as regards length of fame, the above order of precedence may be reversed. But, then, the poet and the composer will come in the end to stand on the same level as the philosopher; since, when once a work is committed to writing, it is possible to preserve it to all time. However, the first place still belongs by right to the philosopher, because of the much greater scarcity of good work in this sphere, and the high importance of it; and also because of the possibility it offers of an almost perfect translation into any language. Sometimes, indeed, it happens that a philosopher's fame outlives even his works themselves; as has happened with Thales, Empedocles, Heraclitus, Democritus, Parmenides, Epicurus and many others.

My remarks are, as I have said, confined to achievements that are not of any material use. Work that serves some practical end, or ministers directly to some pleasure of the senses, will never have any difficulty in being duly appreciated. No first-rate pastry-cook could long remain obscure in any town, to say nothing of having to appeal to posterity.

Under fame of rapid growth is also to be reckoned fame of a false and artificial kind; where, for instance, a book is worked into a reputation by means of unjust praise, the help of friends, corrupt criticism, prompting from above and collusion from below. All this tells upon the multitude, which is rightly presumed to have no power of judging for itself. This sort of fame is like a swimming bladder, by its aid a heavy body may keep afloat. It bears up for a certain time, long or short according as the bladder is well sewed up and blown; but still the air comes out gradually, and the body sinks. This is the inevitable fate of all works which are famous by reason of something outside of themselves. False praise dies away; collusion comes to an end; critics declare the reputation ungrounded; it vanishes, and is replaced by so much the greater contempt. Contrarily, a genuine work, which, having the source of its fame in itself, can kindle admiration afresh in every age, resembles a body of low specific gravity, which always keeps up of its own accord, and so goes floating down the stream of time.

Men of great genius, whether their work be in poetry, philosophy or art, stand in all ages like isolated heroes, keeping up single-handed a desperate struggling against the onslaught of an army of opponents. [7] Is not this characteristic of the miserable nature of mankind? The dullness, grossness, perversity, silliness and brutality of by far the greater part of the race, are always an obstacle to the efforts of the genius, whatever be the method of his art; they so form that hostile army to which at last he has to succumb. Let the isolated champion achieve what he may: it is slow to be acknowledged; it is late in being appreciated, and then only on the score of authority; it may easily fall into neglect again, at any rate for a while. Ever afresh it finds itself opposed by false, shallow, and insipid ideas, which are better suited to that large majority, that so generally hold the field. Though the critic may step forth and say, like Hamlet when he held up the two portraits to his wretched mother, *Have you eyes? Have you eyes*? alas! they have none. When I watch the behavior of a crowd of people in the presence of some great master's work, and mark the manner of their applause, they often remind me of trained monkeys in a show. The monkey's gestures are, no doubt, much like those of men; but now and again they betray that the real inward spirit of these gestures is not in them. Their irrational nature peeps out.

It is often said of a man that *he is in advance of his age*; and it follows from the above remarks that this must be taken to mean that he is in advance of humanity in general. Just because of this fact, a genius makes no direct appeal except to those who are too rare to allow of their ever forming a numerous body at any one period. If he is in this respect not particularly favored by fortune, he will be *misunderstood by his own age*; in other words, he will remain unaccepted until time gradually brings together the voices of those few persons who are capable of judging a work of such high character. Then posterity will say: *This man was in advance of his age*, instead of *in advance of humanity*; because humanity will be glad to lay the burden of its own faults upon a single epoch.

Hence, if a man has been superior to his own age, he would also have been superior to any other; provided that, in that age, by some rare and happy chance, a few just men, capable of judging in the sphere of his achievements, had been born at the same time with him; just as when, according to a beautiful Indian myth, Vischnu becomes incarnate as a hero, so, too, Brahma at the same time appears as the singer of his deeds; and hence Valmiki, Vyasa and Kalidasa are incarnations of Brahma.

In this sense, then, it may be said that every immortal work puts its age to the proof, whether or no it will be able to recognize the merit of it. As a rule, the men of any age stand such a test no better than the neighbors of Philemon and Baucis, who expelled the deities they failed to recognize. Accordingly, the right standard for judging the intellectual worth of any generation is supplied, not by the great minds that make their appearance in it – for their capacities are the work of Nature, and the possibility of cultivating them a matter of chance circumstance – but by the way in which contemporaries receive their works; whether, I mean, they give their applause soon and with a will, or late and in niggardly fashion, or leave it to be bestowed altogether by posterity.

This last fate will be especially reserved for works of a high character. For the happy chance mentioned above will be all the more certain not to come, in proportion as there are few to appreciate the kind of work done by great minds. Herein lies the immeasurable advantage possessed by poets in respect of reputation; because their work is accessible to almost everyone. If it had been possible for Sir Walter Scott to be read and criticised by only some hundred persons, perhaps in his life-time any common scribbler would have been preferred to him; and afterwards, when he had taken his proper place, it would also have been said in his honor that he was *in advance of his age*. But if envy, dishonesty and the pursuit of personal aims are added to the incapacity of those hundred persons who, in the name of their generation, are called upon to pass judgment on a work, then indeed it meets with the same sad fate as attends a suitor who pleads before a tribunal of judges one and all corrupt.

In corroboration of this, we find that the history of literature generally shows all those who made knowledge and insight their goal to have remained unrecognized and neglected, whilst those who paraded with the vain show of it received the admiration of their contemporaries, together with the emoluments.

The effectiveness of an author turns chiefly upon his getting the reputation that he should be read. But by practicing various arts, by the operation of chance, and by certain natural affinities, this reputation is quickly won by a hundred worthless people: while a worthy writer may come by it very slowly and tardily.

The former possess friends to help them; for the rabble is always a numerous body which holds well together. The latter has nothing but enemies; because intellectual superiority is everywhere and under all circumstances the most hateful thing in the world, and especially to bunglers in the same line of work, who want to pass for something themselves.[8]

This being so, it is a prime condition for doing any great work - any work which is to outlive its own age, that a man pay no heed to his contemporaries, their views and opinions, and the praise or blame which they bestow. This condition is, however, fulfilled of itself when a man really does anything great, and it is fortunate that it is so. For if, in producing such a work, he were to look to the general opinion or the judgment of his colleagues, they would lead him astray at every step. Hence, if a man wants to go down to posterity, he must withdraw from the influence of his own age. This will, of course, generally mean that he must also renounce any influence upon it, and be ready to buy centuries of fame by foregoing the applause of his contemporaries.

For when any new and wide-reaching truth comes into the world - and if it is new, it must be paradoxical - an obstinate stand will be made against it as long as possible; nay, people will continue to deny it even after they slacken their opposition and are almost convinced of its truth. Meanwhile it goes on quietly working its way, and, like an acid, undermining everything around it. From time to time a crash is heard; the old error comes tottering to the ground, and suddenly the new fabric of thought stands revealed, as though it were a monument just uncovered. Everyone recognizes and admires it. To be sure, this all comes to pass for the most part very slowly. As a rule, people discover a man to be worth listening to only after he is gone; their *hear, hear,* resounds when the orator has left the platform.

Works of the ordinary type meet with a better fate. Arising as they do in the course of, and in connection with, the general advance in contemporary culture, they are in close alliance with the spirit of their age - in other words, just those opinions which happen to be prevalent at the time. They aim at suiting the needs of the moment. If they have any merit, it is soon recognized; and they gain currency as books which reflect the latest ideas. Justice, nay, more than justice, is done to them. They afford little scope for envy; since, as was said above, a man will praise a thing only so far as he hopes to be able to imitate it himself.

But those rare works which are destined to become the property of all mankind and to live for centuries, are, at their origin, too far in advance of the point at which culture happens to stand, and on that very account foreign to it and the spirit of their own time. They neither belong to it nor are they in any connection with it, and hence they excite no interest in those who are dominated by it. They belong to another, a higher stage of culture, and a time that is still far off. Their course is related to that of ordinary works as the orbit of Uranus to the orbit of Mercury. For the moment they get no justice done to them. People are at a loss how to treat them; so they leave them alone, and go their own snail's pace for themselves. Does the worm see the eagle as it soars aloft?

Of the number of books written in any language about one in 100,000 forms a part of its real and permanent literature. What a fate this one book has to endure before it outstrips those 100,000 and gains its due place of honor! Such a book is the work of an extraordinary and eminent mind, and therefore it is specifically different from the others; a fact which sooner or later becomes manifest.

Let no one fancy that things will ever improve in this respect. No! the miserable constitution of humanity never changes, though it may, to be sure, take somewhat varying forms with every generation. A distinguished mind seldom has its full effect in the life-time of its possessor; because, at bottom, it is completely and properly understood only by minds already akin to it.

As it is a rare thing for even one man out of many millions to tread the path that leads to immortality, he must of necessity be very lonely. The journey to posterity lies through a horribly dreary region, like the Lybian desert, of which, as is well known, no one has any idea who has not seen it for himself. Meanwhile let me before all things recommend the traveler to take light baggage with him; otherwise he will have to throw away too much on the road. Let him never forget the words of Balthazar Gracian: *lo bueno si breve, dos vezes bueno* – good work is doubly good if it is short. This advice is specially applicable to my own countrymen.

Compared with the short span of time they live, men of great intellect are like huge buildings, standing on a small plot of ground. The size of the building cannot be seen by anyone, just in front of it; nor, for an analogous reason, can the greatness of a genius be estimated while he lives. But when a century has passed, the world recognizes it and wishes him back again.

If the perishable son of time has produced an imperishable work, how short his own life seems compared with that of his child! He is like Semela or Maia – a mortal mother who gave birth to an immortal son; or, contrarily, he is like Achilles in regard to Thetis. What a contrast there is between what is fleeting and what is permanent! The short span of a man's life, his necessitous, afflicted, unstable existence, will seldom allow of his seeing even the beginning of his immortal child's brilliant career; nor will the father himself be taken for that which he really is. It may be said, indeed, that a man whose fame comes after him is the reverse of a nobleman, who is preceded by it.

However, the only difference that it ultimately makes to a man to receive his fame at the hands of contemporaries rather than from posterity is that, in the former case, his admirers are separated from him by space, and in the latter by time. For even in the case of contemporary fame, a man does not, as a rule, see his admirers actually before him. Reverence cannot endure close proximity; it almost always dwells at some distance from its object; and in the presence of the person revered it melts like butter in the sun. Accordingly, if a man is celebrated with his contemporaries, nine-tenths of those amongst whom he lives will let their esteem be guided by his rank and fortune; and the remaining tenth may perhaps have a dull consciousness of his high qualities, because they have heard about him from remote quarters. There is a fine Latin letter of Petrarch's on this incompatibility between reverence and the presence of the person, and between fame and life. It comes second in his *Epistolae familiares?* [9] and it is addressed to Thomas Messanensis. He there observes, amongst other things, that the learned men of his age all made it a rule to think little of a man's writings if they had even once seen him.

Since distance, then, is essential if a famous man is to be recognized and revered, it does not matter whether it is distance of space or of time. It is true that he may sometimes hear of his fame in the one case, but never in the other; but still, genuine and great merit may make up for this by confidently anticipating its posthumous fame. Nay, he who produces some really great thought is conscious of his connection with coming generations at the very moment he conceives it; so that he feels the extension of his existence through centuries and thus lives *with* posterity as well as *for* it. And when, after enjoying a great man's work, we are seized with admiration for him, and wish him back, so that we might see and speak with him, and have him in our possession, this desire of ours is not unrequited; for he, too, has had his longing for that posterity which will grant the recognition, honor, gratitude and love denied by envious contemporaries.

If intellectual works of the highest order are not allowed their due until they come before the tribunal of posterity, a contrary fate is prepared for certain brilliant errors which proceed from men of talent, and appear with an air of being well grounded. These errors are defended with so much acumen and learning that they actually become famous with their own age, and maintain their position at least during their author's lifetime. Of this sort are many false theories and wrong criticisms; also poems and works of art, which exhibit some false taste or mannerism favored by contemporary prejudice. They gain reputation and currency simply because no one is yet forthcoming who knows how to refute them or otherwise prove their falsity; and when he appears, as he usually does, in the next generation, the glory of these works is brought to an end. Posthumous judges, be their decision favorable to the appellant or not, form the proper court for quashing the verdict of contemporaries. That is why it is so difficult and so rare to be victorious alike in both tribunals.

The unfailing tendency of time to correct knowledge and judgment should always be kept in view as a means of allaying anxiety, whenever any grievous error appears, whether in art, or science, or practical life, and gains ground; or when some false and thoroughly perverse policy of movement is undertaken and receives applause at the hands of men. No one should be angry, or, still less, despondent; but simply imagine that the world has already abandoned the error in question, and now only requires time and experience to recognize of its own accord that which a clear vision detected at the first glance.

When the facts themselves are eloquent of a truth, there is no need to rush to its aid with words: for time will give it a thousand tongues. How long it may be before they speak, will of course depend upon the difficulty of the subject and the plausibility of the error; but come they will, and often it would be of no avail to try to anticipate them. In the worst cases it will happen with theories as it happens with affairs in practical life; where sham and deception, emboldened by success, advance to greater and greater lengths, until discovery is made almost inevitable. It is just so with theories; through the blind confidence of the blockheads who broach them, their absurdity reaches such a pitch that at last it is obvious even to the dullest eye. We may thus say to such people: *the wilder your statements, the better.*

There is also some comfort to be found in reflecting upon all the whims and crotchets which had their day and have now utterly vanished. In style, in grammar, in spelling, there are false notions of this sort which last only three or four years. But when the errors are on a large scale, while we lament the brevity of human life, we shall in any case, do well to lag behind our own age when we see it on a downward path. For there are two ways of not keeping on a level with the times. A man may be below it; or he may be above it.

NOTES

1. *Welt als Wille*, Vol. II. c. 37.
2. Collier, one of his critical editors, in his Introduction to the Sonettes, remarks upon this point: "In many of them are to be found most remarkable indications of self-confidence and of assurance in the immortality of his verses, and in this respect the author's opinion was constant and uniform. He never scruples to express it,... and perhaps there is no writer of ancient or modern times who, for the quantity of such writings left behind him, has so frequently or so strongly declared that what he had produced in this department of poetry 'the world would not willingly let die.'"
3. *Works and Days*, 293.
4. *The Prince*, ch. 22.
5. Plutarch, *Apophthegms*.
6. *Translator's Note*. - August Mahlmann (1771-1826), journalist, poet and story-writer. His *Herodes vor Bethlehem* is a parody of Kotzebue's *Hussiten vor Naumburg*.
7. *Translator's Note*. - At this point Schopenhauer interrupts the thread of his discourse to speak at length upon an example of false fame. Those who are at all acquainted with the philosopher's views will not be surprised to find that the writer thus held up to scorn is Hegel; and readers of the other volumes in this series will, with the translator, have had by now quite enough of the subject. The passage is therefore omitted.
8. If the professors of philosophy should chance to think that I am here hinting at them and the tactics they have for more than thirty years pursued toward my works, they have hit the nail upon the head.
9. In the Venetian edition of 1492.

ON GENIUS

No difference of rank, position, or birth, is so great as the gulf that separates the countless millions who use their head only in the service of their belly, in other words, look upon it as an instrument of the will, and those very few and rare persons who have the courage to say: No! it is too good for that; my head shall be active only in its own service; it shall try to comprehend the wondrous and varied spectacle of this world, and then reproduce it in some form, whether as art or as literature, that may answer to my character as an individual. These are the truly noble, the real *noblesse* of the world. The others are serfs and go with the soil – *glebae adscripti*. Of course, I am here referring to those who have not only the courage, but also the call, and therefore the right, to order the head to quit the service of the will; with a result that proves the sacrifice to have been worth the making. In the case of those to whom all this can only partially apply, the gulf is not so wide; but even though their talent be small, so long as it is real, there will always be a sharp line of demarcation between them and the millions.[1]

The works of fine art, poetry and philosophy produced by a nation are the outcome of the superfluous intellect existing in it.

For him who can understand aright – *cum grano salis* – the relation between the genius and the normal man may, perhaps, be best expressed as follows: A genius has a double intellect, one for himself and the service of his will; the other for the world, of which he becomes the mirror, in virtue of his purely objective attitude towards it. The work of art or poetry or philosophy produced by the genius is simply the result, or quintessence, of this contemplative attitude, elaborated according to certain technical rules.

The normal man, on the other hand, has only a single intellect, which may be called *subjective* by contrast with the *objective* intellect of genius. However acute this subjective intellect may be - and it exists in very various degrees of perfection - it is never on the same level with the double intellect of genius; just as the open chest notes of the human voice, however high, are essentially different from the falsetto notes. These, like the two upper octaves of the flute and the harmonics of the violin, are produced by the column of air dividing itself into two vibrating halves, with a node between them; while the open chest notes of the human voice and the lower octave of the flute are produced by the undivided column of air vibrating as a whole. This illustration may help the reader to understand that specific peculiarity of genius which is unmistakably stamped on the works, and even on the physiognomy, of him who is gifted with it. At the same time it is obvious that a double intellect like this must, as a rule, obstruct the service of the will; and this explains the poor capacity often shown by genius in the conduct of life. And what specially characterizes genius is that it has none of that sobriety of temper which is always to be found in the ordinary simple intellect, be it acute or dull.

The brain may be likened to a parasite which is nourished as a part of the human frame without contributing directly to its inner economy; it is securely housed in the topmost story, and there leads a self-sufficient and independent life. In the same way it may be said that a man endowed with great mental gifts leads, apart from the individual life common to all, a second life, purely of the intellect. He devotes himself to the constant increase, rectification and extension, not of mere learning, but of real systematic knowledge and insight; and remains untouched by the fate that overtakes him personally, so long as it does not disturb him in his work. It is thus a life which raises a man and sets him above fate and its changes. Always thinking, learning, experimenting, practicing his knowledge, the man soon comes to look upon this second life as the chief mode of existence, and his merely personal life as something subordinate, serving only to advance ends higher than itself.

An example of this independent, separate existence is furnished by Goethe. During the war in the Champagne, and amid all the bustle of the camp, he made observations for his theory of color; and as soon as the numberless calamities of that war allowed of his retiring for a short time to the fortress of Luxembourg, he took up the manuscript of his *Farbenlehre*. This is an example which we, the salt of the earth, should endeavor to follow, by never letting anything disturb us in the pursuit of our intellectual life, however much the storm of the world may invade and agitate our personal environment; always remembering that we are the sons, not of the bondwoman, but of the free. As our emblem and coat of arms, I propose a tree mightily shaken by the wind, but still bearing its ruddy fruit on every branch; with the motto *Dum convellor mitescunt*, or *Conquassata sed ferax*.

That purely intellectual life of the individual has its counterpart in humanity as a whole. For there, too, the real life is the life of the *will*, both in the empirical and in the transcendental meaning of the word. The purely intellectual life of humanity lies in its effort to increase knowledge by means of the sciences, and its desire to perfect the arts. Both science and art thus advance slowly from one generation to another, and grow with the centuries, every race as it hurries by furnishing its contribution. This intellectual life, like some gift from heaven, hovers over the stir and movement of the world; or it is, as it were, a sweet-scented air developed out of the ferment itself – the real life of mankind, dominated by will; and side by side with the history of nations, the history of philosophy, science and art takes its innocent and bloodless way.

The difference between the genius and the ordinary man is, no doubt, a *quantitative* one, in so far as it is a difference of degree; but I am tempted to regard it also as *qualitative*, in view of the fact that ordinary minds, notwithstanding individual variation, have a certain tendency to think alike. Thus on similar occasions their thoughts at once all take a similar direction, and run on the same lines; and this explains why their judgments constantly agree – not, however, because they are based on truth. To such lengths does this go that certain fundamental views obtain amongst mankind at all times, and are always being repeated and brought forward anew, whilst the great minds of all ages are in open or secret opposition to them.

A genius is a man in whose mind the world is presented as an object is presented in a mirror, but with a degree more of clearness and a greater distinction of outline than is attained by ordinary people. It is from him that humanity may look for most instruction; for the deepest insight into the most important matters is to be acquired, not by an observant attention to detail, but by a close study of things as a whole. And if his mind reaches maturity, the instruction he gives will be conveyed now in one form, now in another. Thus genius may be defined as an eminently clear consciousness of things in general, and therefore, also of that which is opposed to them, namely, one's own self.

The world looks up to a man thus endowed, and expects to learn something about life and its real nature. But several highly favorable circumstances must combine to produce genius, and this is a very rare event. It happens only now and then, let us say once in a century, that a man is born whose intellect so perceptibly surpasses the normal measure as to amount to that second faculty which seems to be accidental, as it is out of all relation to the will. He may remain a long time without being recognized or appreciated, stupidity preventing the one and envy the other. But should this once come to pass, mankind will crowd round him and his works, in the hope that he may be able to enlighten some of the darkness of their existence or inform them about it. His message is, to some extent, a revelation, and he himself a higher being, even though he may be but little above the ordinary standard.

Like the ordinary man, the genius is what he is chiefly for himself. This is essential to his nature: a fact which can neither be avoided nor altered, he may be for others remains a matter of chance and of secondary importance. In no case can people receive from his mind more than a reflection, and then only when he joins with them in the attempt to get his thought into their heads; where, however, it is never anything but an exotic plant, stunted and frail.

In order to have original, uncommon, and perhaps even immortal thoughts, it is enough to estrange oneself so fully from the world of things for a few moments, that the most ordinary objects and events appear quite new and unfamiliar. In this way their true nature is disclosed. What is here demanded cannot, perhaps, be said to be difficult; it is not in our power at all, but is just the province of genius.

By itself, genius can produce original thoughts just as little as a woman by herself can bear children. Outward circumstances must come to fructify genius, and be, as it were, a father to its progeny.

The mind of genius is among other minds what the carbuncle is among precious stones: it sends forth light of its own, while the others reflect only that which they have received. The relation of the genius to the ordinary mind may also be described as that of an idio-electrical body to one which merely is a conductor of electricity.

The mere man of learning, who spends his life in teaching what he has learned, is not strictly to be called a man of genius; just as idio-electrical bodies are not conductors. Nay, genius stands to mere learning as the words to the music in a song. A man of learning is a man who has learned a great deal; a man of genius, one from whom we learn something which the genius has learned from nobody. Great minds, of which there is scarcely one in a hundred millions, are thus the lighthouses of humanity; and without them mankind would lose itself in the boundless sea of monstrous error and bewilderment.

And so the simple man of learning, in the strict sense of the word - the ordinary professor, for instance - looks upon the genius much as we look upon a hare, which is good to eat after it has been killed and dressed up. So long as it is alive, it is only good to shoot at.

He who wishes to experience gratitude from his contemporaries, must adjust his pace to theirs. But great things are never produced in this way. And he who wants to do great things must direct his gaze to posterity, and in firm confidence elaborate his work for coming generations. No doubt, the result may be that he will remain quite unknown to his contemporaries, and comparable to a man who, compelled to spend his life upon a lonely island, with great effort sets up a monument there, to transmit to future sea-farers the knowledge of his existence. If he thinks it a hard fate, let him console himself with the reflection that the ordinary man who lives for practical aims only, often suffers a like fate, without having any compensation to hope for; inasmuch as he may, under favorable conditions, spend a life of material production, earning, buying, building, fertilizing, laying out, founding, establishing, beautifying with daily effort and unflagging zeal, and all the time think that he is working for himself; and yet in the end it is his descendants who reap the benefit of it all, and sometimes not even his descendants. It is the same with the man of genius; he, too, hopes for his reward and for honor at least; and at last finds that he has worked for posterity alone. Both, to be sure, have inherited a great deal from their ancestors.

The compensation I have mentioned as the privilege of genius lies, not in what it is to others, but in what it is to itself. What man has in any real sense lived more than he whose moments of thought make their echoes heard through the tumult of centuries?

Perhaps, after all, it would be the best thing for a genius to attain undisturbed possession of himself, by spending his life in enjoying the pleasure of his own thoughts, his own works, and by admitting the world only as the heir of his ample existence. Then the world would find the mark of his existence only after his death, as it finds that of the Ichnolith.[2]

It is not only in the activity of his highest powers that the genius surpasses ordinary people. A man who is unusually well-knit, supple and agile, will perform all his movements with exceptional ease, even with comfort, because he takes a direct pleasure in an activity for which he is particularly well-equipped, and therefore often exercises it without any object. Further, if he is an acrobat or a dancer, not only does he take leaps which other people cannot execute, but he also betrays rare elasticity and agility in those easier steps which others can also perform, and even in ordinary walking. In the same way a man of superior mind will not only produce thoughts and works which could never have come from another; it will not be here alone that he will show his greatness; but as knowledge and thought form a mode of activity natural and easy to him, he will also delight himself in them at all times, and so apprehend small matters which are within the range of other minds, more easily, quickly and correctly than they. Thus he will take a direct and lively pleasure in every increase of Knowledge, every problem solved, every witty thought, whether of his own or another's; and so his mind will have no further aim than to be constantly active. This will be an inexhaustible spring of delight; and boredom, that spectre which haunts the ordinary man, can never come near him.

Then, too, the masterpieces of past and contemporary men of genius exist in their fullness for him alone. If a great product of genius is recommended to the ordinary, simple mind, it will take as much pleasure in it as the victim of gout receives in being invited to a ball. The one goes for the sake of formality, and the other reads the book so as not to be in arrear. For La Bruyère was quite right when he said: *All the wit in the world is lost upon him who has none.* The whole range of thought of a man of talent, or of a genius, compared with the thoughts of the common man, is, even when directed to objects essentially the same, like a brilliant oil-painting, full of life, compared with a mere outline or a weak sketch in water-color.

All this is part of the reward of genius, and compensates him for a lonely existence in a world with which he has nothing in common and no sympathies. But since size is relative, it comes to the same thing whether I say, Caius was a great man, or Caius has to live amongst wretchedly small people: for Brobdingnack and Lilliput vary only in the point from which they start. However great, then, however admirable or instructive, a long posterity may think the author of immortal works, during his lifetime he will appear to his contemporaries small, wretched, and insipid in proportion. This is what I mean by saying that as there are three hundred degrees from the base of a tower to the summit, so there are exactly three hundred from the summit to the base. Great minds thus owe little ones some indulgence; for it is only in virtue of these little minds that they themselves are great.

Let us, then, not be surprised if we find men of genius generally unsociable and repellent. It is not their want of sociability that is to blame. Their path through the world is like that of a man who goes for a walk on a bright summer morning. He gazes with delight on the beauty and freshness of nature, but he has to rely wholly on that for entertainment; for he can find no society but the peasants as they bend over the earth and cultivate the soil. It is often the case that a great mind prefers soliloquy to the dialogue he may have in this world. If he condescends to it now and then, the hollowness of it may possibly drive him back to his soliloquy; for in forgetfulness of his interlocutor, or caring little whether he understands or not, he talks to him as a child talks to a doll.

Modesty in a great mind would, no doubt, be pleasing to the

world; but, unluckily, it is a *contradictio in adjecto*. It would compel a genius to give the thoughts and opinions, nay, even the method and style, of the million preference over his own; to set a higher value upon them; and, wide apart as they are, to bring his views into harmony with theirs, or even suppress them altogether, so as to let the others hold the field. In that case, however, he would either produce nothing at all, or else his achievements would be just upon a level with theirs. Great, genuine and extraordinary work can be done only in so far as its author disregards the method, the thoughts, the opinions of his contemporaries, and quietly works on, in spite of their criticism, on his side despising what they praise. No one becomes great without arrogance of this sort. Should his life and work fall upon a time which cannot recognize and appreciate him, he is at any rate true to himself; like some noble traveler forced to pass the night in a miserable inn; when morning comes, he contentedly goes his way.

A poet or philosopher should have no fault to find with his age if it only permits him to do his work undisturbed in his own corner; nor with his fate if the corner granted him allows of his following his vocation without having to think about other people.

For the brain to be a mere laborer in the service of the belly, is indeed the common lot of almost all those who do not live on the work of their hands; and they are far from being discontented with their lot. But it strikes despair into a man of great mind, whose brain-power goes beyond the measure necessary for the service of the will; and he prefers, if need be, to live in the narrowest circumstances, so long as they afford him the free use of his time for the development and application of his faculties; in other words, if they give him the leisure which is invaluable to him.

It is otherwise with ordinary people: for them leisure has no value in itself, nor is it, indeed, without its dangers, as these people seem to know. The technical work of our time, which is done to an unprecedented perfection, has, by increasing and multiplying objects of luxury, given the favorites of fortune a choice between more leisure and culture upon the one side, and additional luxury and good living, but with increased activity, upon the other; and, true to their character, they choose the latter, and prefer champagne to freedom. And they are consistent in their choice; for, to them, every exertion of the mind which does not serve the aims of the will is folly. Intellectual effort for its own sake, they call eccentricity. Therefore, persistence in the aims of the will and the belly will be concentricity; and, to be sure, the will is the centre, the kernel of the world.

But in general it is very seldom that any such alternative is presented. For as with money, most men have no superfluity, but only just enough for their needs, so with intelligence; they possess just what will suffice for the service of the will, that is, for the carrying on of their business. Having made their fortune, they are content to gape or to indulge in sensual pleasures or childish amusements, cards or dice; or they will talk in the dullest way, or dress up and make obeisance to one another. And how few are those who have even a little superfluity of intellectual power! Like the others they too make themselves a pleasure; but it is a pleasure of the intellect. Either they will pursue some liberal study which brings them in nothing, or they will practice some art; and in general, they will be capable of taking an objective interest in things, so that it will be possible to converse with them. But with the others it is better not to enter into any relations at all; for, except when they tell the results of their own experience or give an account of their special vocation, or at any rate impart what they have learned from some one else, their conversation will not be worth listening to; and if anything is said to them, they will rarely grasp or understand it aright, and it will in most cases be opposed to their own opinions. Balthazar Gracian describes them very strikingly as men who are not men - *hombres che non lo son*. And Giordano Bruno *says* the same thing: *What a difference there is in having to do with men compared with those who are only made in their image and likeness*![3] And how wonderfully this passage agrees with that remark in the Kurral: *The common people look like men but I have never seen anything quite like them.* If the reader will consider the extent to which these ideas agree in thought and even in expression, and in the wide difference between them in point of date and nationality, he cannot doubt but that they are at one with the facts of life. It was certainly not under the influence of those passages that, about twenty years ago, I tried to get a snuff-box made, the lid of which should have two fine chestnuts represented upon it, if possible in mosaic; together with a leaf which was to show that they were horse-chestnuts. This symbol was meant to keep the thought constantly before my mind. If anyone wishes for entertainment, such as will prevent him feeling solitary even when he is alone, let me recommend the company of dogs, whose moral and intellectual qualities may almost afford delight and gratification.

Still, we should always be careful to avoid being unjust. I am often surprised by the cleverness, and now and again by the stupidity of my dog; and I have similar experiences with mankind. Countless times, in indignation at their incapacity, their total lack of discernment, their bestiality, I have been forced to echo the old complaint that folly is the mother and the nurse of the human race:

Humani generis mater nutrixque profecto Stultitia est.

But at other times I have been astounded that from such a race there could have gone forth so many arts and sciences, abounding in so much use and beauty, even though it has always been the few that produce them. Yet these arts and sciences have struck root, established and perfected themselves: and the race has with persistent fidelity preserved Homer, Plato, Horace and others for thousands of years, by copying and treasuring their writings, thus saving them from oblivion, in spite of all the evils and atrocities that have happened in the world. Thus the race has proved that it appreciates the value of these things, and at the same time it can form a correct view of special achievements or estimate signs of judgment and intelligence. When this takes place amongst those who belong to the great multitude, it is by a kind of inspiration. Sometimes a correct opinion will be formed by the multitude itself; but this is only when the chorus of praise has grown full and complete. It is then like the sound of untrained voices; where there are enough of them, it is always harmonious.

Those who emerge from the multitude, those who are called men of genius, are merely the *lucida intervalla* of the whole human race. They achieve that which others could not possibly achieve. Their originality is so great that not only is their divergence from others obvious, but their individuality is expressed with such force, that all the men of genius who have ever existed show, every one of them, peculiarities of character and mind; so that the gift of his works is one which he alone of all men could ever have presented to the world. This is what makes that simile of Ariosto's so true and so justly celebrated: *Natura lo fece e poi ruppe lo stampo.* After Nature stamps a man of genius, she breaks the die.

But there is always a limit to human capacity; and no one can be a great genius without having some decidedly weak side, it may even be, some intellectual narrowness. In other words, there will foe some faculty in which he is now and then inferior to men of moderate endowments. It will be a faculty which, if strong, might have been an obstacle to the exercise of the qualities in which he excels. What this weak point is, it will always be hard to define with any accuracy even in a given case. It may be better expressed indirectly; thus Plato's weak point is exactly that in which Aristotle is strong, and *vice versa;* and so, too, Kant is deficient just where Goethe is great.

Now, mankind is fond of venerating something; but its veneration is generally directed to the wrong object, and it remains so directed until posterity comes to set it right. But the educated public is no sooner set right in this, than the honor which is due to genius degenerates; just as the honor which the faithful pay to their saints easily passes into a frivolous worship of relics. Thousands of Christians adore the relics of a saint whose life and doctrine are unknown to them; and the religion of thousands of Buddhists lies more in veneration of the Holy Tooth or some such object, or the vessel that contains it, or the Holy Bowl, or the fossil footstep, or the Holy Tree which Buddha planted, than in the thorough knowledge and faithful practice of his high teaching. Petrarch's house in Arqua; Tasso's supposed prison in Ferrara; Shakespeare's house in Stratford, with his chair; Goethe's house in Weimar, with its furniture; Kant's old hat; the autographs of great men; these things are gaped at with interest and awe by many who have never read their works. They cannot do anything more than just gape.

The intelligent amongst them are moved by the wish to see the objects which the great man habitually had before his eyes; and by a strange illusion, these produce the mistaken notion that with the objects they are bringing back the man himself, or that something of him must cling to them. Akin to such people are those who earnestly strive to acquaint themselves with the subject-matter of a poet's works, or to unravel the personal circumstances and events in his life which have suggested particular passages. This is as though the audience in a theatre were to admire a fine scene and then rush upon the stage to look at the scaffolding that supports it. There are in our day enough instances of these critical investigators, and they prove the truth of the saying that mankind is interested, not in the *form* of a work, that is, in its manner of treatment, but in its actual matter. All it cares for is the theme. To read a philosopher's biography, instead of studying his thoughts, is like neglecting a picture and attending only to the style of its frame, debating whether it is carved well or ill, and how much it cost to gild it.

This is all very well. However, there is another class of persons whose interest is also directed to material and personal considerations, but they go much further and carry it to a point where it becomes absolutely futile. Because a great man has opened up to them the treasures of his inmost being, and, by a supreme effort of his faculties, produced works which not only redound to their elevation and enlightenment, but will also benefit their posterity to the tenth and twentieth generation; because he has presented mankind with a matchless gift, these varlets think themselves justified in sitting in judgment upon his personal morality, and trying if they cannot discover here or there some spot in him which will soothe the pain they feel at the sight of so great a mind, compared with the overwhelming feeling of their own nothingness.

This is the real source of all those prolix discussions, carried on in countless books and reviews, on the moral aspect of Goethe's life, and whether he ought not to have married one or other of the girls with whom he fell in love in his young days; whether, again, instead of honestly devoting himself to the service of his master, he should not have been a man of the people, a German patriot, worthy of a seat in the *Paulskirche*, and so on. Such crying ingratitude and malicious detraction prove that these self-constituted judges are as great knaves morally as they are intellectually, which is saying a great deal.

A man of talent will strive for money and reputation; but the spring that moves genius to the production of its works is not as easy to name. Wealth is seldom its reward. Nor is it reputation or glory; only a Frenchman could mean that. Glory is such an uncertain thing, and, if you look at it closely, of so little value. Besides it never corresponds to the effort you have made:

Responsura tuo nunquam est par fama labori.

Nor, again, is it exactly the pleasure it gives you; for this is almost outweighed by the greatness of the effort. It is rather a peculiar kind of instinct, which drives the man of genius to give permanent form to what he sees and feels, without being conscious of any further motive. It works, in the main, by a necessity similar to that which makes a tree bear its fruit; and no external condition is needed but the ground upon which it is to thrive.

On a closer examination, it seems as though, in the case of a genius, the will to live, which is the spirit of the human species, were conscious of having, by some rare chance, and for a brief period, attained a greater clearness of vision, and were now trying to secure it, or at least the outcome of it, for the whole species, to which the individual genius in his inmost being belongs; so that the light which he sheds about him may pierce the darkness and dullness of ordinary human consciousness and there produce some good effect.

Arising in some such way, this instinct drives the genius to carry his work to completion, without thinking of reward or applause or sympathy; to leave all care for his own personal welfare; to make his life one of industrious solitude, and to strain his faculties to the utmost. He thus comes to think more about posterity than about contemporaries; because, while the latter can only lead him astray, posterity forms the majority of the species, and time will gradually bring the discerning few who can appreciate him. Meanwhile it is with him as with the artist described by Goethe; he has no princely patron to prize his talents, no friend to rejoice with him:

Ein Fürst der die Talente schätzt, Ein Freund, der sich mit mir ergötzt,
Die haben leider mir gefehlt.

His work is, as it were, a sacred object and the true fruit of his life, and his aim in storing it away for a more discerning posterity will be to make it the property of mankind. An aim like this far surpasses all others, and for it he wears the crown of thorns which is one day to bloom into a wreath of laurel. All his powers are concentrated in the effort to complete and secure his work; just as the insect, in the last stage of its development, uses its whole strength on behalf of a brood it will never live to see; it puts its eggs in some place of safety, where, as it well knows, the young will one day find life and nourishment, and then dies in confidence.

NOTES

1. The correct scale for adjusting the hierarchy of intelligences is furnished by the degree in which the mind takes merely individual or approaches universal views of things. The brute recognizes only the individual as such: its comprehension does not extend beyond the limits of the individual. But man reduces the individual to the general; herein lies the exercise of his reason; and the higher his intelligence reaches, the nearer do his general ideas approach the point at which they become universal.
2. *Translator's Note.* - For an illustration of this feeling in poetry, Schopenhauer refers the reader to Byron's *Prophecy of Dante*: introd. to C. 4.
3. *Opera*: ed. Wagner, 1. 224.

ARTHUR SCHOPENHAUER

By Jeremy Mark Robinson

Arthur Schopenhauer was born in 1788 (on February 22nd) in Gdansk and died in 1860 in Frankfurt (on September 20th). Schopenhauer is known for his major work *The World As Will and Idea*, his philosophy of transcendental idealism, his studies of pessimism, his collections of essays and aphorisms, his incorporation of Eastern religion and metaphysics in his philosophy, and his impressive posthumous influence on philosophers such as Friedrich Nietzsche, Ludwig Wittgenstein, Henri Bergson and Oswald Spengler, psychologists such as Otto Rank, Carl Jung and Sigmund Freud, and a host of writers and artists such as Samuel Beckett, Marcel Proust, Rainer Rilke, André Gide, Hugo von Hoffmansthal, Stéphane Mallarmé, W.B. Yeats, Italo Svevo, Ivan Turgenev, Robert Musil, Jorge Borges, George B. Shaw, Karl Kraus, J.-K. Huysmans, Edgar Allan Poe, August Strindberg, Guy de Maupassant, Frank Wedekind, Antonin Dvorak, Arnold Schönberg, Gustav Mahler, Charles Baudelaire, Jacob Burckhardt, George Gissing, Emile Zola, Richard Wagner, Sergei Prokoviev, Leo Tolstoy, Hermans Melville and Hesse, and Thomases Mann and Hardy.

Arthur Schopenhauer's life was fascinating - which you can read about in many places: the problematic relationship his parents (and his mother in particular), the possible suicide of his father Heinrich (in 1805, aged 58), the women and the love affairs (and prostitutes and illegitimate children and scandals), the studies in Weimar, Berlin, Göttingen and Gotha, his philosophical influences (Plato, Kant, Descartes, Goethe, Aristotle, Locke, etc), his harsh critiques of fellow philosophers[1] (Hegel, Fichte, Schelling, Jacobi), and his dubious views on issues such as race, ethnicity and religion.

Among Arthur Schopenhauer's other works, aside from *The World As Will and Idea,* were *On Vision and Colors, The Art of Being Right, Essays and Aphorisms, Parerga and Paralipomena, On the Basis of Morality, On the Freedom of the Will, On the Will In Nature* and *On the Fourfold Root of the Principle of Sufficient Reason.*

The influence of Arthur Schopenhauer can be discerned in so many places. In literature his influence has been considerable: D.H. Lawrence, Samuel Beckett and Thomas Hardy are obvious examples. What is Hardy's fiction and poetry but the philosophy of Schopenhauer turned into literature? Hardy's novels dragged the famous Schopenhauer pessimism into an English cult of literary miserablism, which crops up in arch, modernist form in the work of Beckett (and even in the pop songs of British acts such as the Smiths, the Cure and New Order). Schopenhauer reminds us that it's OK to be miserable, and to complain about everything.

But Arthur Schopenhauer's work also shallowly plays to (and excuses) life's whingers and miserablists, who see existence as pain, difficulty, and sorrow (just like Buddhism itself, with its dogged emphasis on suffering, and like many strains of Christian theology (the *via negativa*), such as that of St Augustine and Thomas Aquinas, and like some of the Gnostic sects).

It's also that stubborn insistence on life-as-pain of Existential, Nietzschean philosophy: if *I'm* not having a good time, then *no one else* is allowed to have a good time.

Arthur Schopenhauer had his detractors (every philosopher

1 Really good philosophers were thin on the ground, according to Schopenhauer: 'The number of minds in the whole of Europe that are capable of thinking and judging is small'.

does, even Buddha and Jesus) - Bertrand Russell, for example (and Ludwig Wittgenstein changed his mind about Schopenhauer). And today there are many who find his philosophy of pessimism too much, too downbeat, too hopeless.

▼

Arthur Schopenhauer is a clear and entertaining author. He doesn't require footnotes or additional passages to explain what he's trying to say. This makes Schopenhauer very approachable - which isn't always the case with, say, Liebniz, or Kant, or Wittgenstein. Some philosophers require that you not only pay attention (and give 100% of your attention - so put down that cel phone!), you can also follow their complex arguments, step by step.

Arthur Schopenhauer is a one-off among philosophers, a man with a unique worldview and a unique way of getting it across. He is a self-consciously eccentric philosopher. He's not afraid of being cantankerous and difficult. The persona in his essays sometimes resembles a really crabby, old man who just dislikes everything and everybody. He's Scrooge, one of life's misers, who seems to revel in his misery (*he's* right, and *no one* else is allowed to be right. And now *shut up and listen* and he'll tell you why *you're* wrong and *he's* right).

And Arthur Schopenhauer is funny. He's not a gag-a-minute comedy writer, of course, but his dry wit and wry comments help to render his writing appealing.

▼

Arthur Schopenhauer is a grouch at a world-class level: he has raised the art of complaining to a sublime degree. Schopenhauer can rant like few other philosophers. He gets away with it because he is very, very good, and he's a terrific writer or articulator of his thoughts. Being a great thinker is one thing, but being able to put across your philosophy is something else.

It's easy to understand Arthur Schopenhauer's philosophy (most of the time). When he complains about noise, for example ('a daily torment to me all my life long', he gripes in his essay *On*

Noise), many can relate to that (and this was an era before cars, aircraft, motorbikes, television, pop concerts, etc. However, humans have always been noisy).

One of Arthur Schopenhauer's standard tactics is to use the construction of jokes to get across his messages: he will introduce a topic or set up a subject, which seems to take a sentence in one direction, but then he immediately reverses the direction, and adds his own gloss on the subject. This structure resembles jokes – the set-up and the pay-off. The set-up sometimes seems quite ordinary or everyday (and something that many people can identify with), but then comes the pay-off, where Schopenhauer delivers *his* take on a topic.

This form of construction privileges the author, of course (or, in comedy writing, the comedian, or the one scoring the jokes off other people). That is, Schopenhauer places himself on the throne, declaiming on this or that, and scores jokes (or philosophy) off others.

▼

THE ESSAYS.

Arthur Schopenhauer's essays are some of his most approachable works, along with his collections of aphorisms. They are a good place to start with Schopenhauer's philosophy, if the idea of tackling *The World As Will and Idea* seems a little daunting. The authorial voice of Schopenhauer is highly individual, and it revels in its carefully crafted eccentricity.

Arthur Schopenhauer's essays cover a wide range of topics, from anti-social noise to suicide. Indeed, Schopenhauer is one of those thinkers who can talk about pretty much anything – and intelligently and wittily, too. You could give Schopenhauer a subject, and he would be able to speak about it. Even if it was something he knew nothing about, he'd find a way of turning the subject around to something he could use.

Some of the essays are formal, with a logical construction, moving from point to point. Some are rants – Schopenhauer picks up a topic and gets his teeth into it, and won't let it go. Some sound like lectures, but most of Schopenhauer's essays come across as a man talking to some colleagues and friends in an informal setting: the men have retired to a watering-hole in Weimar, Jena or Berlin after dinner, out come the cigars and the pipes (the women have been ushered out, of course), and the talk begins.

Sometimes, the essays sound like someone determined to get his point across to a colleague who insists on being especially argumentative (perhaps because they know that Schopenhauer will take the bait).

Among the topics discussed by Arthur Schopenhauer in his many essays were style and writing • wisdom and knowledge • education • critics and criticism • the notion of genius • psychology • religion • pantheism • books and reading • on thinking for oneself (and not filling your head with secondhand information) • free will • controversy • suicide (perhaps with the fate of his father hanging over him) • morality and ethics • suffering • women • love • and even noise (there's too much noise for Schopenhauer).

In his essay *On Style*, Schopenhauer offers the familiar advice to writers of school teachers and creative writing gurus: be clear, don't be fussy, avoid self-indulgence, leave your ego out of it, don't show off, etc. Schopenhauer derides authors who work for money: true writing, Schopenhauer asserts, is in the service of the subject, not the ego or the dollar.

In essays such as *On Men of Learning* and *On Thinking For Oneself*, Arthur Schopenhauer took a sceptical view of education and universities - even libraries, books and reading.[2] For Schopenhauer, simply consuming information does automatically lead to wisdom: 'information is only a means of insight, and in itself of little or no value', Schopenhauer notes, *pace* the drive to acquire information; rather, 'it is his way of *thinking* that makes a man a philosopher'. 'Students, and learned persons of all sorts and every age, aim as a rule at acquiring *information* rather than

2 He lamented the teaching of Latin disappearing from schools.

insight', he asserted in *On Men of Learning*. Think for yourself is one of Schopenhauer's mantras (explored in the essay *On Thinking For Oneself*), instead of reading or absorbing information for the sake of it (books are second-hand thoughts, someone else's ideas, alien/ foreign notions forced upon the mind).[3] Think, don't read, rely on your own thoughts, not those of others. 'Reading is nothing more than a substitute for thought of one's own', Schopenhauer reckoned. (One can imagine Schopenhauer's reaction to contemporary inventions such as television, chat shows, 'reality' TV, cel phones, the internet, Facebook, and celebrity culture. The idea of watching TV for four hours a day (a typical average in Westernized countries), or using a cel phone (three hours a day on average) would be very alarming for him).

3 So even reading Schopenhauer's books is second-hand information.

SELECT BIBLIOGRAPHY

Some recent books about Arthur Schopenhauer

BIOGRAPHIES

D. Cartwright. *Schopenhauer*, Cambridge University Press, 2010
D. Hamlyn. *Schopenhauer*, Routledge, 1985
J. Matthews. *Schopenhauer's Will*, Nine Point Publishing, 2015
R. Safranksi. *Schopenhauer and the Wild Years of Philosophy*, Weidenfeld & Nicolson, 1989

STUDIES

J. Atwell. *Schopenhauer*, Temple University Press, 1990
—. *Schopenhauer On the Character of the World*, University of California Press, 1995
A. Barua & M. Kossler, eds. *Understanding Schopenhauer Through the Prism of Indian Culture*, De Gruyter, Berlin, 2013
M. Brener. *Schopenhauer and Wagner*, X Libris, 2014
A. Edwards. *An Evolutionary Epistemological Critique of Schopenhauer's Metaphysics*, 123 Books, 2011
A. Hübscher. *The Philosophy of Schopenhauer*, Edwin Mellen Press, 1989
D. Jacquette, ed. *The Philosophy of Schopenhauer*, Acumen, 2005
C. Janaway. *Self and World In Schopenhauer's Philosophy*, Oxford University Press, 1989/ 2003
N. Jordan. *Schopenhauer's Ethics of Patience*, Edwin Mellen Press, 2010
B. Magee. *The Philosophy of Schopenhauer*, Oxford University Press, 1988

G. Mannion. *Schopenhauer, Religion and Morality*, Ashgate, 2003
R. Marcin. *In Search of Schopenhauer's Cat*, Catholic University of America Press, 2006
A. Neil & C. Janaway, eds. *Better Consciousness*, Wiley-Blackwell, 2009
S. Vasalou. *Schopenhauer and the Aesthetic Standpoint*, Cambridge University Press, 2016
B. Vandenabeele. *The Sublime In Schopenhauer's Philosophy*, Macmillan, 2015
E. van der Luft, ed. *Schopenhauer*, Edwin Mellen Press, 1988
R. Wicks. *Schopenhauer*, Blackwell, 2008
—. *Schopenhauer's The World As Will and Representation*, Continuum, 2011
J. Young. *Schopenhauer*, Routledge, 2005

CLASSIC FRENCH FAIRY TALES

Translated and with an Introduction
by Jack Zipes

A collection of 36 classic French fairy tales translated by renowned writer Jack Zipes. *Cinderella, Beauty and the Beast, Sleeping Beauty* and *Little Red Riding Hood* are among the classic fairy tales in this amazing book.
Includes illustrations from fairy tale collections.
Jack Zipes has written and published widely on fairy tales.

'Terrific... a succulent array of 17th and 18th century 'salon' fairy tales'
- *The New York Times Book Review*

'These tales are adventurous, thrilling in a way fairy tales are meant to be... The translation from the French is modern, happily free of archaic and hyperbolic language... a fine and sophisticated collection' - *New York Tribune*

'Enjoyable to read... a unique collection of French regional folklore' - *Library Journal*

'Charming stories accompanied by attractive pen-and-ink drawings' - *Chattanooga Times*

Introduction and illustrations 612pp. ISBN 9781861712510 Pbk ISBN 9781861713193 Hbk

In the Dim Void

Samuel Beckett's Late Trilogy: *Company, Ill Seen, Ill Said* and *Worstward Ho*

by Gregory Johns

This book discusses the luminous beauty and dense, rigorous poetry of Samuel Beckett's late works, *Company, Ill Seen, Ill Said* and *Worstward Ho*. Gregory Johns looks back over Beckett's long writing career, charting the development from the *Molloy-Malone Dies-Unnamable* trilogy through the 'fizzles' of the 1960s to the elegiac lyricism of the *Company* series. Johns compares the trilogy with late plays such as *Ghosts, Footfalls* and *Rockaby.*

Bibliography, notes. Illustrated. 120pp

ISBN 9781861712974 Pbk and ISBN 9781861712608 Hbk
9781861713407 E-book

CRESCENT MOON PUBLISHING

web: www.crmoon.com e-mail: cresmopub@yahoo.co.uk

ARTS, PAINTING, SCULPTURE

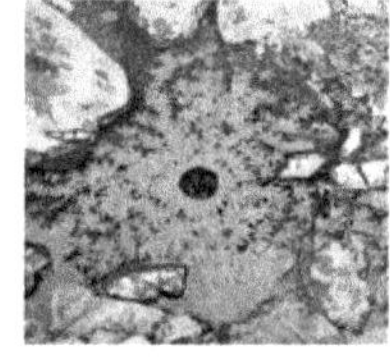

The Art of Andy Goldsworthy
Andy Goldsworthy: Touching Nature
Andy Goldsworthy in Close-Up
Andy Goldsworthy: Pocket Guide
Andy Goldsworthy In America
Land Art: A Complete Guide
The Art of Richard Long
Richard Long: Pocket Guide
Land Art In the UK
Land Art in Close-Up
Land Art In the U.S.A.
Land Art: Pocket Guide
Installation Art in Close-Up
Minimal Art and Artists In the 1960s and After
Colourfield Painting
Land Art DVD, TV documentary
Andy Goldsworthy DVD, TV documentary
The Erotic Object: Sexuality in Sculpture From Prehistory to the Present Day
Sex in Art: Pornography and Pleasure in Painting and Sculpture
Postwar Art
Sacred Gardens: The Garden in Myth, Religion and Art
Glorification: Religious Abstraction in Renaissance and 20th Century Art
Early Netherlandish Painting
Leonardo da Vinci
Piero della Francesca
Giovanni Bellini
Fra Angelico: Art and Religion in the Renaissance
Mark Rothko: The Art of Transcendence
Frank Stella: American Abstract Artist
Jasper Johns
Brice Marden
Alison Wilding: The Embrace of Sculpture
Vincent van Gogh: Visionary Landscapes
Eric Gill: Nuptials of God
Constantin Brancusi: Sculpting the Essence of Things
Max Beckmann
Caravaggio
Gustave Moreau
Egon Schiele: Sex and Death In Purple Stockings
Delizioso Fotografico Fervore: Works In Process 1
Sacro Cuore: Works In Process 2
The Light Eternal: J.M.W. Turner
The Madonna Glorified: Karen Arthurs

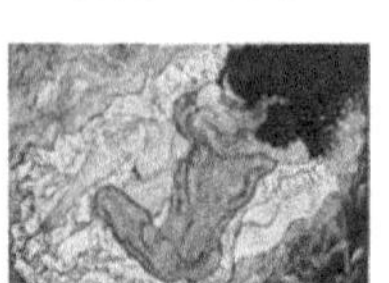

LITERATURE

J.R.R. Tolkien: The Books, The Films, The Whole Cultural Phenomenon
J.R.R. Tolkien: Pocket Guide
Tolkien's Heroic Quest
The *Earthsea* Books of Ursula Le Guin
Beauties, Beasts and Enchantment: Classic French Fairy Tales
German Popular Stories by the Brothers Grimm
Philip Pullman and *His Dark Materials*
Sexing Hardy: Thomas Hardy and Feminism
Thomas Hardy's *Tess of the d'Urbervilles*
Thomas Hardy's *Jude the Obscure*
Thomas Hardy: The Tragic Novels
Love and Tragedy: Thomas Hardy
The Poetry of Landscape in Hardy
Wessex Revisited: Thomas Hardy and John Cowper Powys
Wolfgang Iser: Essays and Interviews
Petrarch, Dante and the Troubadours
Maurice Sendak and the Art of Children's Book Illustration
Andrea Dworkin
Cixous, Irigaray, Kristeva: The *Jouissance* of French Feminism
Julia Kristeva: Art, Love, Melancholy, Philosophy, Semiotics and Psychoanalysis
Hélene Cixous I Love You: The *Jouissance* of Writing
Luce Irigaray: Lips, Kissing, and the Politics of Sexual Difference
Peter Redgrove: Here Comes the Flood
Peter Redgrove: Sex-Magic-Poetry-Cornwall
Lawrence Durrell: Between Love and Death, East and West
Love, Culture & Poetry: Lawrence Durrell
Cavafy: Anatomy of a Soul
German Romantic Poetry: Goethe, Novalis, Heine, Hölderlin
Feminism and Shakespeare
Shakespeare: Love, Poetry & Magic
The Passion of D.H. Lawrence
D.H. Lawrence: Symbolic Landscapes
D.H. Lawrence: Infinite Sensual Violence
Rimbaud: Arthur Rimbaud and the Magic of Poetry
The Ecstasies of John Cowper Powys
Sensualism and Mythology: The Wessex Novels of John Cowper Powys
Amorous Life: John Cowper Powys and the Manifestation of Affectivity (H.W. Fawkner)
Postmodern Powys: New Essays on John Cowper Powys (Joe Boulter)
Rethinking Powys: Critical Essays on John Cowper Powys
Paul Bowles & Bernardo Bertolucci
Rainer Maria Rilke
Joseph Conrad: *Heart of Darkness*
In the Dim Void: Samuel Beckett
Samuel Beckett Goes into the Silence
André Gide: Fiction and Fervour
Jackie Collins and the Blockbuster Novel
Blinded By Her Light: The Love-Poetry of Robert Graves
The Passion of Colours: Travels In Mediterranean Lands
Poetic Forms

POETRY

Ursula Le Guin: Walking In Cornwall
Peter Redgrove: Here Comes The Flood
Peter Redgrove: Sex-Magic-Poetry-Cornwall
Dante: Selections From the Vita Nuova
Petrarch, Dante and the Troubadours
William Shakespeare: Sonnets
William Shakespeare: Complete Poems
Blinded By Her Light: The Love-Poetry of Robert Graves
Emily Dickinson: Selected Poems
Emily Brontë: Poems
Thomas Hardy: Selected Poems
Percy Bysshe Shelley: Poems
John Keats: Selected Poems
Joh n Keats: Poems of 1820
D.H. Lawrence: Selected Poems
Edmund Spenser: Poems
Edmund Spenser: Amoretti
John Donne: Poems
Henry Vaughan: Poems
Sir Thomas Wyatt: Poems
Robert Herrick: Selected Poems
Rilke: Space, Essence and Angels in the Poetry of Rainer Maria Rilke
Rainer Maria Rilke: Selected Poems
Friedrich Hölderlin: Selected Poems
Arseny Tarkovsky: Selected Poems
Arthur Rimbaud: Selected Poems
Arthur Rimbaud: A Season in Hell
Arthur Rimbaud and the Magic of Poetry
Novalis: Hymns To the Night
German Romantic Poetry
Paul Verlaine: Selected Poems
Elizaethan Sonnet Cycles
D.J. Enright: By-Blows
Jeremy Reed: Brigitte's Blue Heart
Jeremy Reed: Claudia Schiffer's Red Shoes
Gorgeous Little Orpheus
Radiance: New Poems
Crescent Moon Book of Nature Poetry
Crescent Moon Book of Love Poetry
Crescent Moon Book of Mystical Poetry
Crescent Moon Book of Elizabethan Love Poetry
Crescent Moon Book of Metaphysical Poetry
Crescent Moon Book of Romantic Poetry
Pagan America: New American Poetry

MEDIA, CINEMA, FEMINISM and CULTURAL STUDIES

J.R.R. Tolkien: The Books, The Films, The Whole Cultural Phenomenon
J.R.R. Tolkien: Pocket Guide
The *Lord of the Rings* Movies: Pocket Guide
The Cinema of Hayao Miyazaki
Hayao Miyazaki: *Princess Mononoke*: Pocket Movie Guide
Hayao Miyazaki: *Spirited Away*: Pocket Movie Guide
Tim Burton : Hallowe'en For Hollywood
Ken Russell
Ken Russell: *Tommy*: Pocket Movie Guide
The Ghost Dance: The Origins of Religion
The Peyote Cult
Cixous, Irigaray, Kristeva: The *Jouissance* of French Feminism
Julia Kristeva: Art, Love, Melancholy, Philosophy, Semiotics and Psychoanalysis
Luce Irigaray: Lips, Kissing, and the Politics of Sexual Difference
Hélene Cixous I Love You: The *Jouissance* of Writing
Andrea Dworkin
'Cosmo Woman': The World of Women's Magazines
Women in Pop Music
HomeGround: The Kate Bush Anthology
Discovering the Goddess (Geoffrey Ashe)
The Poetry of Cinema
The Sacred Cinema of Andrei Tarkovsky
Andrei Tarkovsky: Pocket Guide
Andrei Tarkovsky: *Mirror*: Pocket Movie Guide
Andrei Tarkovsky: *The Sacrifice*: Pocket Movie Guide
Walerian Borowczyk: Cinema of Erotic Dreams
Jean-Luc Godard: The Passion of Cinema
Jean-Luc Godard: *Hail Mary*: Pocket Movie Guide
Jean-Luc Godard: *Contempt*: Pocket Movie Guide
Jean-Luc Godard: *Pierrot le Fou*: Pocket Movie Guide
John Hughes and Eighties Cinema
Ferris Bueller's Day Off: Pocket Movie Guide
Jean-Luc Godard: Pocket Guide
The Cinema of Richard Linklater
Liv Tyler: Star In Ascendance
Blade Runner and the Films of Philip K. Dick
Paul Bowles and Bernardo Bertolucci
Media Hell: Radio, TV and the Press
An Open Letter to the BBC
Detonation Britain: Nuclear War in the UK
Feminism and Shakespeare
Wild Zones: Pornography, Art and Feminism
Sex in Art: Pornography and Pleasure in Painting and Sculpture
Sexing Hardy: Thomas Hardy and Feminism

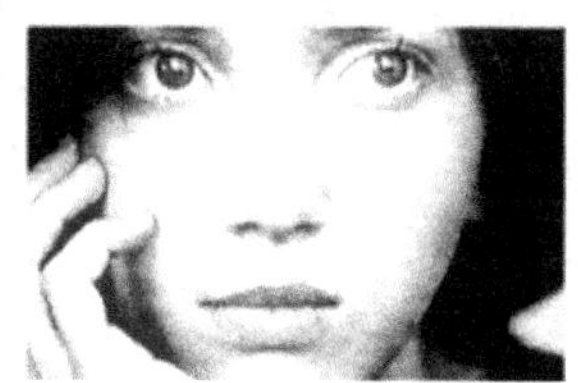

The Light Eternal is a model monograph, an exemplary job. The subject matter of the book is beautifully organised and dead on beam. (Lawrence Durrell)
It is amazing for me to see my work treated with such passion and respect. (Andrea Dworkin)

CRESCENT MOON PUBLISHING
P.O. Box 1312, Maidstone, Kent, ME14 5XU, Great Britain. www.crmoon.com

cresmopub@yahoo.co.uk   www.crescentmoon.org.uk

www.ingramcontent.com/pod-product-compliance
Lightning Source LLC
LaVergne TN
LVHW050536100826
845148LV00002B/581

* 9 7 8 1 8 6 1 7 1 9 0 0 3 *